# VISUAL PARABLES

## ENGAGING THE SPIRITUAL ELEMENTS OF FILM

Institute of the Southwest Publishing Division

Thousand Oaks, California

# A MODERN TEXT FOR

# CHRISTIAN PARENTS, EDUCATORS

# AND CLERGY

**To my children**

*Film per se is just celluloid strips . . . it becomes art when a choice is made to employ it for aesthetic ends.   When those ends . . . are regarded as worth trying for, a movie becomes an end in itself, a vehicle by which the human spirit becomes free.*

*Man and the Movies*, 17

# CONTENTS

# PREFACE

*Visual Parables* is designed to offer parents, teachers and clergy a modern perspective on film as a source of spiritual growth, values education and social responsibility.  It is the author's hope that the resources shared in these chapters may become tools for renewal and for guiding youth toward mature Christian values and an appreciation of their own unique place in society.

In the author's experience, the journey into the world of film art is both personal and universal.  Through the reflective process it is possible to appreciate film's capacity to serve as parable and teach a moral lesson.  By exploring a film's aesthetics and themes and applying them for personal growth and motivation for social action, the human spirit may be enriched.

Since film is a component of mass media, it shares some of the traits of television, news, and advertising.  The messages the media send tend to be absorbed passively unless they are met with critical thought.  Becoming an active viewer and "reading the images" which are on the screen guarantee that the individual will not be manipulated by the medium, but rather informed and enriched by it.

In order to enhance the readers' spiritual journey, a few tips on how to read images and improve your visual literacy will be discussed in Chapter 2. Use this information to develop an active method of interacting with the films you see. As you watch a movie, you will identify the images, comprehend their literal meaning and discover how they are used in context. Then you will be able to teach your children or students to do the same!

Outfitted with the basics of visual literacy, you are prepared to engage the spiritual process. Discovering the art of a film and its ideology will enlighten and draw the viewer into the spiritual context of the work. Once engaged in the spiritual milieu, the viewer can consider the values presented, accept or reject them, and offer oppositional readings which the viewer believes to be socially or spiritually constructive.

While all films which are produced are not socially or

spiritually redeeming, value may be found in carefully selected mainstream and independent motion pictures. A selective listing and short description of the subject and/or themes of such films can be found in the Appendix. It is recommended that repeated screenings be employed when examining these films for the purpose of spiritual enrichment, as their metaphorical representations are not always readily identifiable with one viewing.

May the reading of film as parable enliven your spirit, challenge your presuppositions, encourage social action, provide a source of values education for your children and bring you joy. Happy viewing!


JM

1997

# 1

## INTRODUCTION

We all love the movies -- perhaps because they take us to exotic locations, engage our fantasies, or simply allow us a temporary respite from the strain and stresses of everyday life. However, on a deeper level, the medium of film is more than popular entertainment; it is also an art form. As an art form, it carries with it the same potential as literature, painting, sculpture and music: the ability to address the universal questions of life and inspire the human spirit.

As a visual medium, film has tremendous power to influence its audience, especially since it has become more realistic in its representations, making it increasingly difficult for the viewer to determine the difference between fantasy and reality. If its representations are constructive, film can be an unlimited source of spiritual growth and serve as a tool for the education of children in their development of a moral and social conscience.

Film at its simplest level is parable: a metaphorical story which teaches us about our collective conscience. Just as Jesus used parables to teach a moral lesson to his followers, so filmmakers employ imaginary storylines as metaphors to discuss themes of importance to the filmmaker. Parables utilize conventions to which the ordinary citizen can relate, as biblical parables such as the prodigal son and the mustard seed employed. Such conventions or stereotypes were easily comprehended by the masses because of their cultural relevance.

Through the aesthetics, codes and conventions of filmmaking and the development of narrative and character, motion pictures have the potential to reveal elements of truth, confront us with our weaknesses, present us with moral dilemmas, and move us to social action. While many social critics believe that movies are a destructive influence in society, there are numerous films produced each year which ennoble, illuminate and inspire, as well as provide us with insights into ourselves and how we relate to the world.

Narrative and action are the devices filmmakers employ to reach the audience. These devices function to reveal an ideology, a social or political concern, and to stimulate an emotional response from the viewer in order for he or she to "buy-in" to the characters and the storyline. It is through this emotional awakening that the audience is drawn into the world on the screen. If the filmmaker has brought depth and wisdom to the material and to the characters, the seeds have been sown for an intellectual and/or spiritual reflection to take place.

Furthermore, film is a medium of illusion, simulating reality and stretching itself continuously to illustrate the appearance of reality. Film is a journey into an imaginary world of actors, facades, celluloid edits and special effects. But it is precisely that illusion that gives film its mystical quality and its spiritual relevance. Behind the illusions, the possibility of discovery and rediscovery of elementary truths relative to human purpose linger.

As in other forms of storytelling, film engages archetypal, mythical characters and situations. For example, in Native American oral tradition, the coyote often serves as an archetypal figure in a cultural context. The animal is a culturally-derived symbol which has meaning to Native Americans but whose meaning is lost to non-Natives. In addition to serving as the principal character in a story, the coyote is involved in a situation which is meant to reveal a spiritual truth, an ancestral bond, or a moral lesson.

Similarly in film, mythical characters are created and reinvented with the repetition of a genre. In American film, such characters include the action hero, the cowboy, the detective, the femme-fatale -- characters culturally-derived and ideologically consistent with American myths and conventions. Our obsession with these characters speaks to us of our values as they reveal deeper psychological and cultural issues which we may not always view as healthy and may wish to challenge.

To assist readers in understanding how to address the spiritual aspects of film, it is suggested that you consider the same principles used in the evaluation of painting, music and literature. These principles include the identification and significance of themes and symbols as well as the exploration of fully developed characters. To approach film in this way presupposes the dignity and worth of individuals and their capacity for self-realization and growth.

As the reader begins to consider film as a spiritual tool, it is suggested that the following questions be used for reflection:

1.	Did the film provoke a powerful emotional response either for or against the film?

2.	What was the film's theme?  Was it important?  Did it challenge me in any way?

3.	What does the film tell me about the culture it represents, values, ethnic or gender relationships?

4.      What is the basic storyline, and how does it metaphorically represent a moral issue or inform the spirit?

5.      Were the characters multi-dimensional and how did they inspire or confront my presuppositions and values?

6.      How did the cinematic aspects of the film (photography, lighting, music, editing, etc.) promote or enhance its spiritual message?

7.      Does the film encourage social action?  If so, in what way?

8.      Does the film evoke an appreciation of the creative life force?

9.      Is there a respect for nature, human life and human endeavor supported in the film?

10.     How does the film make me feel about myself, others, and the world around me?

11.     Is the film gratuitous in its representations of sex and violence or does it respect the dignity of its characters?

12.     Does the film exploit a person, group or ideology, or does

it help me to understand more fully the beliefs and culture of others?

13. How does the film propose that I should relate to others, to a superior being, to an afterlife?

## REDEFINING THE SPIRITUAL

Before beginning our journey into the spirituality of film, it is important to define what is meant in this text by "spiritual." When one reflects on spiritual experiences, it is not unlikely that consideration is often restricted to those encounters which engage prayer, meditation, contemplation, and art forms or literary works which speak of the religious. Specific environments, as well, are usually associated with the spiritual, such as the seashore, the mountains, churches, synagogues, temples, shrines and other places of worship.

In addition to the Old and New Testaments, the Torah, the Koran, the Book of Mormon, and the lives of the saints, hundreds of books on discernment and spirituality have been written to

motivate the individual to seek perfection and to do good in the

community. Spiritual directors and mentors from all faiths help

individuals examine their lives in order to enhance their

understanding of their place in the world and their relationship

with a higher being or with the universe.

Christians have been taught to stay close to that which

elevates and to avoid that which degrades humanity in order to be

"spiritual" people. In the process, individuals have become judges

of what is "good" and what is "evil," in some ways limiting their

experiences rather than trusting their prayerful discernment to

guide them through the more complex and darker recesses of life.

Christians are aware that confining "spirituality" to

churches and prayer groups will not engage social problems. In

order to help create a more just and humane society, the individual

must bring spirituality to action. Since film provides the viewer

with a mirror of social as well as personal issues, its reflections are sources of insights into the problems of society and the nature of humankind. Just as important, film raises the consciousness about self in relation to society in the privacy of one's own heart.

It is important to recognize that films which depict violence and inhumanity are not necessarily lacking in a spiritual dimension. On the contrary, they may inspire viewers to action and growth in ways they never would have expected. We can be disturbed and be spiritually engaged; we can be horrified and be moved to social reform. We can come away from a film in tears because we have seen ourselves so clearly in a character and yearn for our own redemption. We can emerge from a film experience enraged and have it motivate us to change the course of our lives. Thus, when engaging in the spiritual context of film evaluation, it is important to open ourselves to any experience. By watching film characters confront their conflicts, make their choices and suffer the consequences, the audience unconsciously renders its own moral choices. In this way viewers are both educated and challenged.

The controversial film, *Indecent Proposal*, made its commercial success on the examination of a moral dilemma, in effect asking viewers to consider whether they would commit adultery for $1 million. While this film's storyline was based on the social and psychological issues associated with this choice, i.e., "God," "the commandments" or "personal virtue" were not issues here, it nevertheless, offered its viewers insights into the values of American society. The film is based on the assumption that personal decision-making in American society takes place in the absence of a moral code. How this film and its agenda are read, and how these themes personally affect the way in which individuals see themselves and the world form the basis for the viewer's spiritual growth.

*Indecent Proposal* is a film for mature audiences and certainly is not family fare. However, the moral issues presented in the film might be useful as a basis for personal evaluation, group discussion, or the education of teens.  Literally, *Indecent Proposal* can be read as a film about greed, prostitution, temptation, and adultery.  But the story works as parable, and these themes symbolize the struggle the characters endure when faced with choices which must be made devoid of a moral code. Integrity, commitment and fidelity, along with one's inability to "buy" love at any price, underlie the superficial motivations of the characters in the film.  *Indecent Proposal* then becomes a statement about the "absence" of moral courage and commitment in a society consumed by greed.

Films written with themes which are in themselves uplifting or which present the audience with moral dilemmas, such as *Indecent Proposal*, are beacons to the viewer to become spiritually engaged in the text.  It is only necessary to look, listen and critically assess what is seen and heard, taking into the soul what is food and tossing away what is chaff.

If lives are enriched by film experiences, it is because the individual is in touch with the human condition, which is never perfect and often reprehensible. To deny one's participation in one's culture is to deny a sense of community, and to deny a sense of community is to deny the life of the spirit.

# 2

# UNDERSTANDING FILM

It is not a difficult task to comprehend the themes of most American feature films, and frankly many of us unconsciously evaluate and pass judgment on the movies we see without ever really thinking about it. Therefore, this chapter should only reinforce what you already know: how to identify, define and understand film images.

## MEDIA LITERACY

Over the past twenty years or so, the academic community has discussed the importance of educating ourselves and our children to be alert and active in relation to media messages. Thus, media studies and the terms "media literacy" and "visual literacy" have evolved. Four principles which are essential to understanding how to read images are noted below.[1]

1.     *Media construct reality*

Media do more than record or reflect reality; they actually construct it.  Considine and Haley note in *Visual Messages*

*Although the images and the stories may seem real, or "true to life," they are always structured to represent a particular point of view, perspective, ideology, or value system.*[2]

"Reading images" requires deconstructing this apparent reality, i.e., breaking the images down by identifying them, analyzing them and evaluating them.

2.     *Media use identifiable techniques*

The film industry utilizes production techniques, film language, codes and conventions which we can learn to identify and understand.

3.     *Media are businesses with commercial interests*

The film industry, as other media, is in business to make money.  Commerciality most often drives decision-making.  A viewer can ask the obvious questions: who makes money from this? how is it tailored to increase profit?


4.     *Media present ideologies and value messages*

Certain images and ideologies predominate, because they create the possibility of a more commercially successful product, i.e., they appeal to a larger group of individuals in the mass audience who buy-in to the ideology being presented.  Consider the association of characters with patriotic symbols such as the flag.  This association teaches or reinforces the value that "nationalism is good."  Consider the use of images of pretty or sexually alluring women in film, suggesting that women are decorations or objects of desire.  The value which is reinforced is that "women should be pretty or sexually attractive."  Once we identify the themes, we can adopt oppositional readings by accepting or rejecting the implied ideology of the image.

Media literacy is not censorship as it does not have a moral agenda. It teaches awareness, merely providing tools for analysis. Viewers filter media experiences through their own cultural screens, which sort, accept and reject certain values and conventions. From there, the viewer as parent, educator or clergy can decide how to teach children to read "images" and provide opportunities for discussion and moral training. Oppositional readings can be developed in a family, church or youth group setting, thereby reinforcing values which are deemed appropriate.

## VIEWING FILM AS ART

In order to appreciate the artistic as well as spiritual dimensions of film, the viewer must become familiar with the language of filmmaking. Over time viewers assimilate the cultural conventions and contexts associated with them and they become unconscious.  In other words, you know them, you just don't know you know them!

### Mise-en-scene

Film art may be understood through the concept of **mise-en-scene**, a French term borrowed from the theater which refers to the arrangement of all the visual elements of a theatrical production within a given space -- the stage.[3]

Don't let this fancy term scare you!  In lay person's language, by analyzing the composition of the frame, that is, the lighting, props, position of the characters, posture of the characters in relation to other persons or objects, and the point of view of the camera, the audience can ascertain the mood and meaning these factors cumulatively create.  Then the viewer can apply what he or she perceives to an understanding of the whole narrative.

Analysis of a shot or scene for symbolism and meaning begins with:

**Posture and position** (of the characters).

How are the actors placed in the scene? In relation to each other? Is one actor sitting while another actor is standing? Are both actors in the same position at the same level? This analysis helps us determine who has the power in the scene. Watch *Dangerous Liaisons*. Note the position of John Malkovich in relation to Glenn Close through scene after scene, especially on the staircases. The power positions support the dialogue and the dynamics of their relationship at a given moment.

**Point of view**

Point of view refers to the camera position. Is the action taking place from the point of view of an actor's own vision (subjective camera) or is the camera recording action as if it were a third party? (objective)

**Props**

What props are used in the scene? Where are they located in relation to the actors? What message do they send?

**Place**

In what setting is the action or dialogue shot?  In *Quiz Show*, director Robert Redford provides a salient example of the effective use of "place."  Redford explained that he shot the scene where Van Doran confesses his deed to his father in an academic setting to emphasize that "corruption had come to academe."

Other films recommended for mise-en-scene analysis include: *Ordinary People, Citizen Kane, Rebel Without A Cause, Age of Innocence, Dead Poets Society.*

## VIEWING FILM AS IDEOLOGY

All films have a purpose which is intended by the filmmaker and an ideology which may or may not be intended. Among the purposes of film can be included: profit, entertainment, escapism, propaganda (cultural or political manipulation or indoctrination), social and/or political reform, artistic expression, education, dramatization of human interest stories, historical events or figures.

The ideology supported by a film is more complex, and it can be studied through the film's genre or in isolation.

American films usually fall within established conventions or formulas which are called genres. A **genre** is a story type or category of story types -- a loose set of expectations exploring recurring story patterns and myths typical of a given culture or period. The stylized conventions and archetypal story patterns of genre films encourage the audience to participate ritualistically in the basic beliefs, fears, and anxieties of our culture and era.

Filmmakers like genres because they automatically synthesize a vast amount of iconographical (symbolic) information which frees the director to explore more personal concerns. In a non-generic movie, the artist must communicate all the major ideas and emotions within the work itself. The genre artist builds upon the accomplishments of predecessors, enriching their ideas or calling them into question. In addition, genres adapt to changing social conditions.  Examples of genres include: westerns, musicals, thrillers, science fiction/fantasy, war films, Kungfu, love stories, horror, film noir, gangster films, epics, crime drama, biopic, action/adventure films, comedies, prison films.

### The Western

The western genre is a mainstay of American filmmaking, a formula to which we can all relate.  Westerns are often vehicles for exploring clashes of values between Eastern and Western America.  Some of the common elements found in westerns include:

**Era and location**. Westerns take place in the western part of the United States in the late 19th century.

**Characters** always include a sheriff or lawman, an outlaw, saloon keeper, dancehall girl (sometimes prostitute), banker, doctor, unmarried school teacher, gambler, scout, hero/loner, preacher, the cavalry, cowboys, Indians, gunfighters.

The physical **Setting** of the story usually takes place in a town, on a ranch, prairie, in the mountains, an Indian village, jail, or fort.

**Plots** contain a showdown/shootout, cattle rustling, jail break, cleaning up a corrupt town, the gold rush, an Indian attack, a journey of wagon trains or pioneers, struggle between farmers and ranchers.  Most westerns depict the arrival of hero who will bring some semblance of order, justice, or redemption to the lives of the characters.[4]

**Props** include black and white hats or horses which are common conventions used to convey "good guys versus bad guys" or the struggle between good and evil.  All westerns have horses, guns, and a broad landscape.

**Ideology** in westerns most often demonstrates a conflict between East (as represented by wealth, education, aristocracy and citizenship) and West (characterized by lawlessness, struggle to survive the elements, lack of formal or advanced education).  Courage, bravery, isolation, violence as a way of life, physical versus mental labor, the loner male, the sacrificing female, and greed are common themes expressed in westerns.

Note the ideology associated with the western. While it changes slightly with the era and its cultural conventions, the basic formula usually remains. Thus, as we watch a western, we already know the ideology it sells. It is the viewer's task to filter it and determine its value in a spiritual context or as a tool for teaching.

## The Action/Adventure Feature

Turning to another popular genre, the reader will be quick to identify the elements which are usually found in formula action/adventure films.

**Plots** include dangerous situations requiring skill and heroism, fast action sequences usually involving peril for the hero, violence, a quest, and suspense.

**Characters** include a hero (or anti-hero), a villain (usually foreign), a romantic interest and/or sexual encounter.

**Props** include firearms, explosives, cars, trains, and other relatively fast modes of transportation.

**Era, location, and setting.** As opposed to a western, action/adventure films can take place in any era, location, or setting. However, the majority of films seem to take place in a city or on foreign soil.

Consider how the action/adventure genre has been culturally altered in the 1990s in response to women's equality issues. The traditional male action hero has been replaced by the female action hero. Instead of (or in addition to) playing the sexual or romantic interest, the woman now carries a gun or displays her abilities in karate, out-fighting and out-smarting the traditionally male villains. How does this shift in roles reflect the filmmaker's vision of women in contemporary American society? Is it socially constructive and how would you discuss it with your children?

Steven Spielberg is reportedly the most commercially

successful American director of all time.  His action/adventure films, *Raiders of the Lost Ark* and its sequel *Indiana Jones and the Temple of Doom*, were incredibly popular.  The author recommends that the reader rent the videorecordings and rethink these two films in terms of visual literacy, art, ideology and Christian values.  This exercise will not only be valuable in terms of spiritual and socially relevant insights, but also provide you with a hands-on application of a new way for you to reflect on film.  As you view the videorecordings, ask yourself the following questions:

1.      What statement does each film make?

2.      What is the significance of the Ark and how does it represent a religious ideology? (Remember all films have an intended purpose and an ideology which may or may not be intended!)

3.      On another level, is *Raiders* actually an allegory, that is, does it, as a whole, have a hidden meaning or represent

something else?

4.      What American values are supported in the films?

5.      How are sex roles defined or redefined as the movies progress and how is that indicated?

6.      How are foreigners represented and does that make a comment about American values?

7.      Who do you think Jones represents ideologically? Consider his name, his ethnic background, his occupation, his personality, his fears, his relationship with women, and his values as you reflect on the character.

8.      What symbols are used or repeated (motif) throughout the films? What do you think they represent? Example, the whip, snakes, etc.

9.      Overall, what is the point of view of the filmmaker, or what does each film "sell?"

10.     Do you agree with the values and ideologies and American myths represented in these films?

11.    How would you talk to your children or students about

these issues?


Now the reader is ready to take on a few simple film

techniques to assist in the appreciation of the symbolic, often

spiritual meaning of the filmmaker.    After reading the next

chapter, try them out when watching a movie on television or rent

a favorite film so that you can stop the tape and replay a scene to

pick up the deeper symbolism or more subtle themes underlying

the storyline.

# 3

# FILM TECHNIQUES

The film industry successfully operates on three principles: 1) the passive manipulation of the viewer by motion pictures through the operation of such principles as identification, wish fulfillment, vindication and escapism; 2)  the public exposition of personal information about the director or actors in order for the audience to identify with the filmmaker or actor's personal tragedies, and thereby be emotionally tied to the content of the film; 3) promotion of interviews and television programs about the making of the film, so that the viewer feels privy to inside information and thereby has some stake in the success of the film.

The psychological and emotional motivators used by the film industry to increase the probability of commercial success are designed for the mass audience.  The intelligent, visually literate and active viewer, however, is aware of these processes and engages the film experience quite differently.

The active viewer will investigate the text and context of the film in question, ask questions of it and confront its assumptions thereby experiencing the spiritual and social dimensions of the film. If individuals see the storyline as a parable, they automatically consider it metaphorical and search for meaning beneath the surface. It is here that the viewer normally finds the richness and wisdom of the filmmaker.

To inform the reader, five film techniques are included here to assist in the viewer's understanding of film language. In addition, suggestions for reviewing some of these techniques on videorecording will provide the viewer with "experience" in identifying them and their general purpose for application in later film review.

The following techniques are often used to promote metaphorical representations in a film. While there are an unlimited number of ways in which meaning may be inferred, including dialogue, it is the purpose of this chapter to bring to the viewer's attention techniques which are easy to identify and common to the experience.

## THE MOTIF

Often a filmmaker repeats the use of a particular prop, musical theme, or event in order to suggest symbolism. For example, in *Dead Poets Society* the motif of time is represented by the use of props such as clocks, clock towers with chimes and watches, as well as references to time in the dialogue. The underlying meaning of the symbolism can best be understood in light of the overall film, i.e., that time is precious and is marching on. Do not waste it! Thus, the motto "*carpe diem*," seize the day.

Another example of film motif can be explored in *Age of Innocence*, where director Martin Scorcese utilizes the rose obsessively throughout the film as a symbol of a budding love affair which is never consummated.

It is helpful then to be aware of the repetition of elements in a film; there is always a purpose and it is rewarding to discover it!

## MONTAGE AND CROSSCUTTING

Two editing techniques which are often used to allude to a metaphorical meaning include montage and crosscutting, both of which are built on the simple construction of juxtaposition. Another fancy word!  Simply stated, juxtaposition is the process whereby one shot is edited up against another shot for a symbolic purpose.  In *Dead Poets Society*, the shot of a flock of geese is juxtaposed (or edited side by side) with a shot of the students descending a staircase.  The implication is that the students are like the geese in their conformity to their environment.

Another example of juxtaposition is found in *Citizen Kane,* where a screeching bird is edited side by side with a shot of

Kane's wife raving about her unhappy life.

## Montage

The original purpose of montage, as created by Russian filmmaker Sergei Eisenstein, required the juxtaposition of dissimilar shots in a series which would provide some symbolic or intellectual meaning (see *Potemkin*, the Odessa steps sequence). In other words, shots of objects and people and places which logically have no connection to each other are edited together in the classical montage.

However, American and European filmmaking have striking differences, and the intellectual content of film is one of them. Since American filmmaking emphasizes narrative (i.e., horizontal storytelling through a logical progression of time) rather than intellectual exploration (vertical enlargement of an idea), American directors rarely use montage in the way Eisenstein intended.

In American motion pictures, one sees examples of time

montage, i.e., a succession of brief shots which dissolve into each other to compress action and convey the passage of time (see *Hoosiers* or *Rocky I-IV*); memory montage, as in *Rocky IV*, when Rocky Balboa relives significant moments of his life while driving his car; stream of consciousness, where an individual's thoughts are imaged quickly and erratically; in the opening sequence of most American films, where significant elements of the story, i.e., characters, locations, symbols are previewed through a succession of brief shots which dissolve into each other.

## Crosscutting

Crosscutting is a technique which is extremely effective in making a statement in film. It is accomplished by editing two sets of circumstances which are occurring simultaneously against each other. Usually, each set of circumstances is presented in a montage style, i.e., short shots with no dialogue, often dissolving into each other, only images relaying an overall meaning. Then the editor alternates from one location to another, moving back and forth letting each set of circumstances inform the other. The films *Havana* and *Mississippi Burning* provide two excellent examples of crosscutting.

In *Havana*, director Sydney Pollack presents two Havanas: one which is corrupt and supports a hedonistic culture, the other which is idealistic, struggling for human rights and the overthrow of a dictator. In the crosscutting sequence, Pollack shows Jack Weil (Robert Redford) who represents the corrupt Havana in a sexual liaison with two women in his apartment. Simultaneously, the revolutionaries are fighting for their freedom and being killed. Pollack's contrast of the two Havanas living side by side is powerfully enacted by cutting back and forth between the two sequences. In *Havana*, crosscutting serves to place the hedonistic culture as reprehensible in the face of such an important political and social dilemma.

*Mississippi Burning* offers another crosscutting sequence. The FBI has just ordered military troops to assist them in locating three dead civil rights workers.  As the plan moves ahead and the busses filled with support troops are enroute to the site, the director crosscuts to terrorist attacks being made on Black citizens and their churches.  The connection: as a result of the intensified efforts of the FBI, the white supremacists have retaliated and only more deaths will result.  Cause and effect have been established.

## IMAGE TO SOUND RELATIONSHIPS

Image to sound relationships, whether congruent or in counterpoint, are very important to understanding the message of the filmmaker and the spiritual relevance of the film.  The viewer will recall in *Dead Poets Society* the haunting, eerie music which is first encountered when Neil picks up the volume of poetry in his room at Welton Academy.  A variation of that theme continues when the boys go to the cave the first night, appearing like hooded monks, running through the mist.  By preparing the audience for "danger," the filmmaker has foreshadowed the death of Neil Perry.

When Neil is brought home by his father after his acting debut and prepares for his suicide, the theme is repeated.  This is an example of congruent image to sound relationship; the images and the sound support each other.

*Good Morning Vietnam* provides the viewer with an example of counterpoint, where music and images are set in opposition to make a moral statement.  In this particular montage sequence, the film takes the viewer through shots of gunboats, napalmed villages and injured civilians.  The music which is offered in counterpoint to inform the meaning of the sequence is *What A Wonderful World*.

## CAMERA ANGLES

One of the simplest techniques in moving-making involves the position with which the camera encounters the action.  The cultural conventions associated with such a shot involve issues of power.  In a low-angle shot, the camera shoots upward at a figure or object indicating dominance or authority. In contrast, a high-angle shot, in which the camera shoots downward on an object or person creates a sense of smallness or subjugation. A film such as *Dangerous Liaisons* uses camera angles continuously to comment upon the shifting power between the two principal characters.

A tilted angle gives the impression that the person or circumstances being filmed is off center, i.e., in a state of unbalance. A similar effect can be accomplished by using a fish-eye lens, which distorts reality to such an extent that anything viewed through the lens will take on the ambiance of psychological abnormality.

Hopefully, this introduction to symbolic film language will enable the viewer to enjoy the experience of film evaluation at a more meaningful level. The reader is encouraged to view the films mentioned in order to identify more readily with the techniques.

For those readers who have already mastered these basic film techniques and wish to advance that knowledge, a glossary of film terms, techniques and their explanation is provided in the Appendix, along with suggested films and selected scenes for reviewing specific techniques.

# 4

## FILM ANALYSES

Ten films have been chosen to include here both for the purposes of example -- so the reader can use them as guidelines for review or the basis for group discussion -- and the spiritual enrichment of the reader who may be encountering the films for the first time. It is the author's intention to point out themes which are particularly evocative to elevate the movie-going experience for the reader.

The reader will see that some films have been analyzed in greater depth than others due to the complexity of their subtext. Others are quite simple and require only basic review to filter the spiritual issues relevant to this discussion. Further discussion of the simpler films would also destroy the opportunity for readers to discover important narrative or symbolic elements on their own. All the films in this chapter work as "parable."

The reader is asked to pay particular attention to moral issues which are raised, characters who are memorable and inspirational, film aesthetics and production techniques such as cinematography and music which are particularly evocative, and social themes which confront your values or call you to action.

Discussion of the film's themes and characters with others is also helpful, since additional perspectives always enlighten us beyond our own cultural screens and limited experience. It is the hope of the author that this approach to viewing film will be spiritually rewarding.

The reader will gain the most from this exercise by:

1.      Reviewing the questions delineated in Chapter 1;

2.      Screening the film;

3.      Reading the analysis contained in the chapter;

4.      Screening the film a second time.

# FILMS

*Dead Poets Society*

*Out of Africa*

*Falling Down*

*Empire of the Sun*

*The Neverending Story*

*Shadowlands*

*Age of Innocence*

*Searching for Bobby Fischer*

*Nobody's Fool*

*Dead Man Walking*

*Dead Poets Society* (1989) US - Drama

**Synopsis:**

Set in a New England preparatory school in 1959, several students who are preparing for the Ivy League and professional careers meet an unconventional English teacher. Mr. Keating (Robin Williams) breaks through the traditional formula of the educational system at Welton and shows the boys how to enrich their lives through the love of literature and challenges them to listen to their inner voices in order to discover their special gifts.

**Analysis:**

Australian Peter Weir directs a beautifully photographed, inspiring film in *Dead Poets Society*. The director's portrayal of Welton Academy is filled with exterior landscapes, which mirror the psychological tensions of the characters. The themes evolve through the use of personalities in conflict. Through the dialogue of the headmaster, teachers and parents, the viewer quickly learns about the philosophy of education encountered at Welton, unequivocally representing the established social order of the wealthy. All students who are enrolled are expected to excel and become highly respected professionals; all seem to have their futures predestined by their parents in partnership with the academy.

The continuity of this theme is reflected in the shot of Neil Perry's room before his suicide (remember mise-en-scene!). The image of his ordered and thoroughly controlled future lies before him on the bed: his mother has "laid out" in a geometric pattern everything he needs for his stay at home.

John Keating is a new teacher (and former student) at Welton, and he represents an opposing force with which the students must contend. Welton Academy maintains the patriarchal structure which dominates Western culture and education, a structure which uses dominance, fear and intimidation to socialize its students. Keating is by nature a humanist, through whom the students become aware of a personal, inner light and the possibility of an extraordinary encounter with life.

As a role model, Mr. Keating both conforms and does not conform.  His non-conformity is seen in his personality and his teaching style.  He whistles as he walks out of the classroom, smiles, has wit and warmth, and his teaching methods are sometimes unconventional.  Yet Keating reflects a level of acceptance of the patriarchal model, seated with the other teachers at meals, sometimes dressing formally as they do, other days wearing a sweater rather than a coat and tie.  Keating lives within a system which he does not allow to imprison him, respecting the order of it but not its domination.

Keating loves his vocation, because he loves literature.  For him, literature is life constantly renewing itself, and the satisfaction he receives in teaching is the sharing of this life-force. The sensitivity Keating has for the creative side of life is a gift he gives to his students rather than an expectation.  He opens their eyes to other ways of looking at the world (he has them stand on his desk to illustrate the point), and thus frees their imaginations. Each boy is affected at a different level; some radically, some rejecting Keating's philosophy altogether.

Neil Perry finds what he believes is his true voice in acting. Later in the story, however, it becomes apparent that he lacks the maturity necessary to deal effectively with the conflict his passion for acting creates. Rather than lose the approval of a domineering father, he chooses self-destruction.

Knox Overstreet finds courage to seek what he wants and no longer fears the consequences. Todd Anderson, learns that he has value, that what is inside of him is good and worth having. (The classroom scene where Todd is badgered into exposing his inner creative voice is effectively communicated). Charles Dalton becomes so radical in his application of his new-found imagination that he throws out all caution and loses his appreciation for the opportunities that a formal education can provide him.

Keating is blamed for the death of Perry as well as for the actions of the other students whose lives he has impacted, and he is fired. The students are constrained to comply with the demands of the administration and sign a document which implicates Keating in all manner of wrong-doing. Though Keating has inspired them, he has also cautioned the students to be wise about their choices. Two students did not choose to follow his advice. They both suffered destructive consequences: one death, the other expulsion.

The director's use of image to image (juxtaposition) and image to sound relationships to promote the symbolism in the film has been noted in a previous chapter and is repeated here for emphasis. The flocks of geese, which Weir employs as a metaphor, are representative of the conformity of the students' ordered lives. In one scene, a flock of geese is juxtaposed with a cut to the students descending a staircase on their way to class. In a later scene, Knox Overstreet is shown on his bicycle charging down the side of a hill, frightening the geese into scattered flight.

Knox has disturbed the conformity of the flock, just as he has

ventured out of conformity, and is impassioned to try to win the

favor of the girl of his dreams.

An effective use of image to sound occurs when the boys

decide to resurrect the Dead Poets Society and meet in the cave

that first evening.  A sense of mystery and imminent danger is

evoked.  First, we see Neil Perry enter his room and discover a

book of poetry on his desk.  His expression tells us that this book

has mysteriously appeared, and he opens it and reads the

handwritten words of Thoreau, a passage to be invoked at the

beginning of each meeting of the society.  Are we to assume that

Keating has mysteriously placed this book here?  As Neil reads the

inscription, the eerie musical score stirs our curiosity and warns us

of some impending danger.  A variation of this musical theme

continues as we see the hooded figures of the students, running

through the darkness and fog later that evening to meet at the cave, reinforcing a mystical, mysterious aura. The sound of owls and the flight of a bird, unexpectedly rising from the ground, startle the viewer and add to the sense of danger. Here, the editing further enhances the mood through silence and slightly retarded motion to increase the length of this sequence and thereby promote anxiety in the viewer. The audience is being prepared for the destructive consequences of the boys actions and ultimately for Neil Perry's death.

The suicide sequence is compelling in its symbolism as it continues the image to sound relationship. The eerie music prompts our attention, for we recognize the mystical score and we are warned of impending danger. We watch Neil, framed by the open window in his room, place the garland he wore as Puck on his head. As Neil stands bare-chested in the window, the image created is that of the Christ-figure, crowned with thorns before his execution. Neil is being represented as "victim," as the lamb going willingly to his death. After making peace with his decision, Neil slowly descends to his father's office. A cut to the key, the drawer of the desk, and we watch Neil pull the gun, shrouded in a handkerchief, out of the drawer and lay it on the desk. Then Weir artistically pulls us to the climax by what he does not show us. We do not see the suicide or the gun. Weir, instead, cuts to Neil's father as he sits up in bed reacting to the sound of the shot which the audience never hears.

There are two motifs in the film which comment on the metaphorical aspects of the film's themes. As previously mentioned, the director comments on time through the use of clocks, bells and watches. Yet the actual time as far as the plot is concerned is not important. Thus, the time symbols appear to be employed to enhance the theme of order and remind the viewer that time is precious or that time is running out.

The bagpipe is a second motif which is engaged throughout the film. In the opening sequence, a student in procession plays the bagpipe and is seen as part of the established social order. In a later scene, the bagpipe is being played at the edge of the lake in a shot beautifully framed by the trees. The "solitude" of the player and instrument is apparent as the scene cuts to Todd Anderson in his room, desperately trying to write a poem. He is alone in his creating, as the musician is alone on the dock just after sunset. Todd struggles to free himself from the bondage of fear and inadequacy. At the same time the music of the bagpipe creates its tense sound, mimicking Todd's struggle to find his inner voice and at the same time providing a sense of non-conformity or individuality. When the boy rejects his work and discards the paper, the sound of the bagpipe immediately ceases. The simulated sound of bagpipes is again noted in the final scene of the film, but this time it participates in the emotional conclusion as backdrop for the triumph of individualism.

The final scene of the film brings about a proper conclusion, where all the emotions which have been evoked throughout the film come to a climax, and the triumph of the spirit of Keating's philosophy is conveyed.  Keating enters the classroom for the last time in an effort to remove his personal affects.  As Keating nears the door to leave, Todd Anderson attempts to speak to him but is silenced by the Headmaster conducting the class.  In frustration, Todd finds a way to acknowledge his respect and admiration for Keating by standing on his desk, imitating a technique used earlier in the film by Keating as a classroom exercise.  The student, in a daring display of courage and commitment, calls out "Oh Captain, My Captain,"  Keating stops to acknowledge Todd, as many of the other students follow the boy's example.

As the film concludes, only Todd's face is framed through the legs of another student.  As his image lingers on the screen, the viewer feels a proper resolution, knowing that Todd has found the courage to believe in his own voice, and that he will ultimately live a fuller life because of Keating's influence.

**Issues of Spiritual Relevance:**

The spiritual significance of this film lies in its exposure of the emotional and psychological tyranny that is imposed on others by well-meaning authority figures. In addition, the viewer is uplifted by the words of Walt Whitman, Henry David Thoreau, Robert Frost, along with Keating's charm -- then disenchanted when faced with the reality of Neil's untimely death. Through this experience, the film draws the viewer to ponder the validity of one's own existence and choices -- to look upon beauty, romance, love and all the experiences of being human and to evaluate their respective roles in life.

Neil's suicide presents the viewer with a moral dilemma, one which can be addressed spiritually and which would be especially important to discuss with teens.

The audience may also recognize the power of a teacher's influence to encourage and inspire students with an infectious spirit that can pervade their entire lives. The character of John Keating epitomized this benevolent force.

The viewer may come forth from this film with the excitement of seeking unchartered waters, yet with an understanding of the dangers inherent in discarding sensibility and order. The moral code here may be summarized with the simple statement that breaking with tradition may have painful consequences.

The slogan with which Mr. Keating encourages his students, "Carpe diem", i.e., seize the day, reminds the viewer that every individual's time on earth should be something truly extraordinary. The film supports the belief that each person has something special to pursue, and that living involves identifying that "something" and moving toward it.

*Dead Poets Society* validates the dignity of the individual and the individual's special place in the world, as well as the gifts with which one has been bestowed. This film had a marked effect on teenage audiences, encouraging them to find their inner voices and to have the courage to challenge that which is oppressive. It gave teens a sense of hope and optimism about their future, and most important, a sense of self-worth.

*Out of Africa* (1985) US - Drama

**Synopsis:**

The most celebrated film of 1985 was Sydney Pollack's enchanting elegy, *Out of Africa*, which received six academy awards including Best Picture, Best Director, Best Screenplay Adaptation, Sound, Cinematography and Original Score.[5] *Out of Africa* is based on the memoirs of Danish writer Karen Blixen (who published under the name of Isak Dinesen), Judith Thurman's biography *Isak Dinesen: The Life of a Story-Teller*, Errol Trzebinski's biography of Finch Hatton, *Silence Will Speak*, and *Out of Africa* and *Shadows on the Grass* by Isak Dinesen.[6]

From 1913 to 1931, Karen Blixen lived in British East Africa (Kenya), where she ran a large coffee plantation. She originally came to Africa to marry Baron Bror Blixen, the twin brother of the man she really loved.  Once married, Bror and Karen were friends and occasional lovers, but Bror was a philanderer.  Karen contracted syphilis from him, was cured, and finally separated from Bror, remaining on the farm while he pursued his living as a hunter.  After Bror's departure, Karen developed a powerful emotional attachment to Denys Finch Hatton, an English Earl's son.  Denys led wealthy tourists on safaris, hunted on his own, and occasionally visited Karen on her farm.[7]

**Analysis:**

In *Out of Africa*, the relationship between Denys Finch Hatton and Karen Blixen provides the argument for differing views of life.  The director explores the dialectic between freedom and possession, using the love affair as the essential metaphor, and for our purposes, creates a parable of universal significance against the social and political domination of the British in East Africa in the early part of the 20th Century.

We are introduced to Africa as a limitless, untamed world gradually being invaded by the "civilized" elements of society: the colonizers (British), landowners, hunters, trains, jeeps and airplanes.  The Africans are being pushed off their land, employed as servants, farm workers, and guides on the hunt.  Who will "own" and dominate this country is the question posed by the filmmaker and the thread running through the narrative.

As civilization advances and the British continue to rule the affairs of British East Africa, symbols of consumption accompany the political events, lived out in the personal lives of the protagonists.  Syphilis nearly claims Karen's life, consumes her fertility, leaving her with the pain of childlessness.  Fire consumes Karen's coffee crop, leaving her financially broken.  Finally, fire consumes Denys' Finch Hatton's plane, killing him instantly.

The two world views personified by the protagonists are presented for the viewer to evaluate in terms of his/her own values.    Denys Finch Hatton's obsession with freedom is demonstrated in his concern for the African environment and his instinctive respect for the essence of life.  This trait is dramatized when Denys allows a lioness to go unharmed rather than kill her as she approaches Karen in the wild, because he understands the habits and responses of the animal and wishes to preserve nature rather than destroy it.    Ambiguity does arise in his characterization, however, since he also hunts for money.  Denys walks a line between respecting nature and exploiting it, which adds complexity to his personality.

In contrast to Denys, Karen's possessive and controlling instincts rule her, and they are dramatized in her attempts to stop the flow of the river with a dam, restrict the growth of the natural vegetation, conform the servants to her lifestyle (symbolized by forcing a servant to wear white gloves), and force schooling on the native children.  Karen's possessions (her china and her crystal) are concrete representations of her materialistic orientation and her need to "own."

Moreover, Karen's possessive instincts cause her to fear Denys' absence from her. She questions his intentions when Felicity wants to accompany him on a safari, and tells him that she hopes they will marry some day because "she wants to be worth something." Denys balks at her invasion of his freedom, her wifely instinct to mend his shirt, her jealousy over Felicity. As her demands upon him increase, Denys retreats.

Karen's European conventions of love and marriage contradict Denys' philosophy of freedom. Yet his genuine love for her is unmistakable, something which Karen is unable to be satisfied by because of who she is. As modern psychologist, M. Scott Peck, noted in his book on psychology and spirituality, *The Road Less Traveled*:

> *Genuine love not only respects the individuality of the other but actually seeks to cultivate it, even at the risk of*

*separation or loss. The ultimate goal of life remains the spiritual growth of the individual, the solitary journey to peaks that can be climbed only alone.*[8]

In Pollack's version of *Out of Africa*, Denys is capable of genuine love. He continually validates Karen's personal worth and seeks to cultivate her individuality by contributing to her experiences and growth. Rather than stop her from traveling to see her husband, Denys gives her a compass to help her find her way, thus respecting her initiative and bravery. Appreciating her talent as a storyteller, he offers her a pen and encourages her to write down her stories. Denys shares with her a view of Africa in an airplane which teaches her that the human spirit, like the land, is meant to be free. He takes her on a safari, knowing that she will instinctively understand the grace and beauty of the land and its natural inhabitants before it is gone. He brings her a gramophone on which she can enjoy Mozart.

However, it is Denys' inability to part with even a fraction of his own freedom that keeps him imprisoned in his freedom. His relationship with his best friend, Berkeley Cole, demonstrates the man's lack of genuine intimacy with others.

Berkeley is dying.  As Denys asks him if he can take him home to England, Berkeley confesses that he wishes to stay, that he has a female companion, who has lived with him for some time.  Denys is stricken with dismay.  "Why didn't you tell me," he asks Berkeley.  Berkeley replies: "I didn't think I knew you well enough."

The film ends in tragedy as Denys is killed and Karen has lost everything she has valued in her life: her ability to conceive, her husband, her farm, her possessions, and her relationship with Denys.  Accepting the needlessness of ownership, she leaves Kenya and returns alone to Denmark.

**Issues of Spiritual Relevance:**

*Out of Africa* addresses not only our common human struggles with possessiveness, ownership, and the abiding human need to be free, but also the possibility of genuine love.  As the film suggests, genuine love was an ideal that Karen was unable to achieve.  At the same time, though Denys was capable of genuine love, he was fearful of commitment, unable to part with a "piece" of his own freedom in order to align his life with another person.

Ownership and fear of commitment dominate the personalities of Karen and Denys, respectively, and the universal moral questions that arise out of their relationship can be summarized:

Can you live your life without paying any price personally?

Is the greater need the collective one?

How does one reconcile personal freedom with obligation to another or to society?

*Out of Africa* offers visual beauty, enchanting prose,

Mozart and the wisdom of two fascinating characters. There is something of value in this film for everyone as well as lessons to be learned about courage, obligation and responsibility, the meaning of freedom and the power of love.

## *Falling Down* (1991) US - Drama

**Synopsis:**

This existential drama is set in Los Angeles in the 1990s. The protagonist, Bill Foster (Michael Douglas), is a man on the edge of destruction. Alienated from his wife and daughter, Foster attempts to "go home" to celebrate his daughter's birthday. As he walks through the streets of Los Angeles, he is confronted with a variety of conflicts, which serve as microcosms for the examination of social issues in an increasingly dehumanizing urban environment. In his attempts to resist the evil he perceives around him, Foster commits increasingly violent crimes and eventually is hunted down by police in a finale in which he chooses death over continuing to live in a hostile world.

**Analysis:**

Anyone who has lived in Los Angeles can identify with the frustration and alienation which are experienced by Foster.  He is a man who is blocked from fulfillment on every side, imprisoned by an uncaring world.  Foster see his life as meaningless.  His wife has divorced him and has a restraining order against him, which prevents him from seeing his daughter.  He is no longer employed by the defense contractor for whom he worked for years, as his role has become obsolete.  As he moves through the city with the goal of reaching his daughter on her birthday, Foster finds himself surrounded by hostility and uncooperative people.  Disillusioned with every element of society with which he comes in contact, his fragile psyche unravels thread by thread, pushing him to the brink of his own destruction.

The cinematic exposition of Foster's sense of frustration is captured in the opening sequence, where Foster is stuck in traffic on a hot, smoggy day. The first shot frames an extreme close up of Foster's mouth, distorted by the tension he feels. As the camera backs away we see the perspiration forming above his upper lip, then his face. Foster's eyes are dull, and one shot at a time, in montage style, the viewer is pulled into the emotional state of the protagonist who is trapped in his car in a traffic delay. Surrounded by noise, pollution, and obnoxious strangers which become intolerable to him, Foster abandons his car and tries to walk to his destination. The protagonist's sense of entrapment reflected in the claustrophobia-induced microcosm of the traffic jam has set the stage for his rapid deterioration. This is how Foster sees the world.

As Foster begins his journey home, he stops at a convenience store and asks for change so he can make a telephone call. The proprietor, who is Korean, will not give him change, and tells him he must buy something. So Foster reluctantly goes to the refrigerator and picks up a soft drink.  As he attempts to pay for the drink, the proprietor tells him the cost, which will not allow him enough change to make the phone call.  The inhumanity of the proprietor and the greed Foster associates with him causes him to lose his temper, and he breaks up the store with the baseball bat the proprietor keeps for self-defense.

The microcosm created here describes the mistrust associated with cultures living side by side, unable to communicate effectively, increasing the probability of misunderstanding and hostility.  Foster is a product of an earlier era; he wants to return to a time when life was in order, when things were simpler, when the economy was more dependable; when a Coke cost fifty cents. Foster is not only obsolete in his job, he is obsolete in his society.

As he continues through the city, Foster encounters two homeboys who will not allow him to sit down and rest his feet on their turf.  He attempts to talk to them about his situation and asks them to be fair.  After a verbal altercation with them, one of the boys threatens him with a switchblade.  A scuffle ensues, and Foster hits the boys with the bat, then breaks away from them and discards the bat for the switchblade.  In this scenario, the director created a second microcosm dealing with racial/ethnic hostility, this time involving the gang element.

The homeboys won't let the incident pass, and they return to look for him by car, armed with automatic weapons.  The hoods attempt a drive-by shooting, but miss him, and after they crash their car and are seriously injured,  Foster takes their automatic weapons in a gym bag and runs off, but not before deliberately shooting one of the boys in the leg.

Cinematically, the director shows the audience the growing insensitivity in Foster, as he passes those on the street who have been gunned down without showing any concern for them.  In addition, it is the protagonist's first offensive, rather than defensive act as he walks directly to the car and retaliates against the gang members.

Additional scenarios complete the conflicts in this film. The next incident involves the lost art of "customer service." Foster enters a fast-food restaurant, where he asks for breakfast. He is told that breakfast is not served after 11:30 am. It is 11:33. He presses the issue and is met with no cooperation. Finally, he pulls out an automatic weapon, and the manager serves him what he requests. When he is served, Foster is dismayed that the product is inferior to that which is advertised--another betrayal of the consumer!

Next, Foster meets a panhandler in the park with whom he has an argument. The man lies to Foster repeatedly in an attempt to get money from him. Foster eventually tells him to get a job and gives him a briefcase which is empty except for his lunch.

Finally, Foster encounters the world of the white supremacist. He enters an army surplus store to evade the police and to buy a pair of hiking boots. The owner has been listening to the police scanner and is aware of who Foster is. After insulting the gay customers in his store, the owner takes Foster in the back room--thinking the two men share the same views about the government--and shows him his Nazi paraphernalia.  Outraged by the attitudes of the store owner, Foster confronts him, reminding him that this is America where everyone is allowed to disagree.  The owner attacks him in an attempt to turn Foster over to the police.  At first Foster defends himself with the switchblade.  After the store owner has been injured, Foster picks up a gun and murders the man in cold blood.

When Foster leaves the surplus store, he is dressed in combat gear and has taken with him an arsenal of weapons.  He has become a vigilante.  The protagonist has made the transition from victim to predator.

Foster next encounters the deceit of construction workers tieing up traffic to "fix" a road that doesn't need fixing and shoots off a bazooka at a construction site.  He then invades the world of the wealthy, walks through a country club golf course to the ire of the golfers.  The elitist attitude of one golfer irritates Foster, and an argument between them results in an angina  attack.  While the man's nitroglycerin tablets are on the golf cart, Foster has blown away the breaks on the cart and sent it dashing down the hill into a water hole.  Foster shows no compassion for the ailing golfer and walks away, lamenting the fact that the golf course should be turned into a park where families can come and recreate.

Foster's final encounter is at the estate of a plastic surgeon, where he terrorizes the caretaker and his family.  These are kind and gentle people, and Foster does not hurt them.  He merely remarks that the opulence which surrounds him informs him that he went into the wrong profession.

Fear is a dominant emotion in *Falling Down*.  Most of the characters are motivated and/or paralyzed by it.  The police officer's wife lives in a state of dependency and emotional paralysis -- fearful of her husband not coming home alive.  The Korean store owner protects himself with a baseball bat out of fear of attack; the hoods are afraid of Foster who has stumbled on to their territory and use intimidation to try to scare him away. The bystanders and employees of the fast food restaurant are afraid of Foster when he pulls out an automatic weapon and threatens them. The white supremacist store owner shows his fear of difference through his hatred of gays and his racist views. The Latino girl is afraid to tell the police what she has witnessed in the drive-by shooting for fear of retaliation. Foster's ex-wife is so afraid of him that she has a restraining order and calls the police twice to her home after receiving phone calls from him as he made his way to her Venice home.

Emotional balance is provided by the police officer, Prendergast (Robert Duvall). There is irony here, since this is a man who deals with crime and its victims on a daily basis. The viewer expects insensitivity from him. However, he is treated badly at the station by his fellow officers; they dislike him because he does not display the macho facade they expect of him. As his supervisor says: I don't trust a man who doesn't swear!

His last day on the job Prendergast deliberately involves himself in the Foster case, and as he talks to each of the characters, his kindness and respect is delivered in sharp contrast to the bullying techniques used by the other officers. In addition, the relationship between he and his wife is one of unconditional love. His wife has lost her youth, her figure, her child, and she is emotionally unstable. His understanding, patience and love for her are so genuine and remarkable that the redemptive quality of their relationship is the only thing holding up hope in this film.

The climax of the film brings Foster to a standoff with Prendergast. These two alter-egos and their world views collide. As a result of the twisted nightmare of his life and misfortunes, Foster has become the "bad guy," the criminal, the hunted. He is astounded that he has become what he has despised. He tells the officer he spent his life building missiles, defending his country and following all the rules. He states: "I did what I was told; I should be rewarded." Foster's realization that those in power lie and manipulate is understood and underscored by Prendergast who admits: "They even lie to the fish!"

**Issues of Spiritual/Social Relevance:**

Alienation, fear and unconditional love are the principal themes underlying the film. Foster is alienated from society, his employer, his family, as are many of the other characters in the film. Unable to adapt to the changes he perceives in his urban environment, Foster becomes increasingly violent and more criminal in his behavior.

Foster's appearance and his room give us clues about his personality and underscore his obsolescence. His clothes, his glass frames and his hairstyle all point to a man who is lost in a prior generation.

Foster's psyche is further exposed through his conflicts as the narrative progresses, and the viewer learns more about his values, and what it is he "de-fens."   Foster moves from a state of

contained anger to successive levels of violence ending in murder

and suicide.

*Falling Down* is a reality check.  The film questions our

social relationships and our values.  On a universal level, the film

relates the urban nightmare which is so prevalent in the

contemporary world: cities torn apart by mistrust, hatred, poverty

and joblessness and the destruction of the individual's dignity and

humanity in the process.  From the filmmaker's point of view,

only the economically viable survive in this society -- it all comes

down to money.  The inevitable destruction of human beings "who

played by all the rules" is presented as a consequence of the reality

of urban living in the 1990s.

This insight is a direct assault on the myth of the

"American Dream."  Part of the mythology associated with the

American Dream involves the faithful, hard-working individual,

who plays by the rules of society and is rewarded for loyalty and service.  The myth bespeaks fairness, but for Foster, it delivers disillusionment and despair.  This consequence forces the viewer to ask the question: Who benefits in society these days?  Is anyone "secure"?

While the audience sees the homeless, gangsters, immigrants and others personified in *Falling Down* as obvious victims of the system, it may disturb the viewer to see the middle class character, portrayed by Michael Douglas, dehumanized by the system as well.

The title of the film is appropriate, in that the filmmaker asks the viewer if society is truly spiraling downward into self-destruction.  There are many issues to reflect upon in the film, and the viewer will certainly experience the hopelessness with which many of the characters are invested, as well as the possibility of unconditional love.

One of the more powerful calls to social action, *Falling Down* presents the audience with a world nearly devoid of spiritual vision and light. *Falling Down* is reminiscent of other films in its genre such as *Grand Canyon* and *Boyz n the Hood*, which are highly recommended for their insights into urban reality in the final decade of the 20th century.

*Empire of the Sun* (1987)- US - Drama

**Synopsis:**

*Empire of the Sun* was directed by Steven Spielberg and adapted from J.G. Ballard's best selling autobiographical novel. The film takes place in Shanghai prior to the beginning of, and during, World War II. The protagonist is Jim Graham (Christian Bale), a young British boy who is separated from his parents as the Japanese invade Shanghai. The story relates his experiences under Japanese captivity.

In summary the parable reads as follows:  Jim is a privileged boy of British parents, growing up in Shanghai in 1939. The British occupy Shanghai and are invested in its economy.  In contrast, the Chinese are poor and maintain the smaller businesses in the city or live in squalor in the country.

Jim and his family are ready to leave Shanghai as the Japanese invade the city in 1939.  Separated from his parents during the initial attack, Jim wanders the city expecting to be treated with privilege by the Japanese soldiers because he is British.  On the contrary, they ignore or mock him.  He returns to his home where he hopes his parents will come to rescue him.  Eventually, running out of food and water, he decides to leave his home.  On the road Jim sees Brits being trucked to holding camps and attempts to join them.  Too weak to catch up, he wanders the city of Shanghai and eventually encounters two American mercenaries who take him into their care, hoping to use him for economic gain.

When Jim and Basie (John Malkovich) are captured by the Japanese, they are taken to a holding camp, where everyone is sick and dying from dysentery.  Basie becomes Jim's tutor in survival.

Jim trusts Basie, learns quickly from him and becomes self-reliant.

Jim, Basie and other prisoners are soon moved to an internment

camp.   During his internment, Jim discovers way to ingratiate

himself to the other prisoners, both American and British, as well

as the Japanese commander of the camp.   He survives, helps

others to survive, and eventually is reunited with his parents when

the war ends and the camp is liberated.


**Analysis and Issues of Spiritual Relevance:**

There is an abundance of subtext in this story and it is

heavily laden with spiritual themes.  Due to the integrity of the

issues, the analysis will not be separated from the discussion of

spiritual issues in the film.

*Empire of the Sun* challenges the viewer to reflect upon

such issues as the existence of God, the disparity between wealth

and poverty, the essence of the "enemy" as evil, and the

willingness to lay down one's life for another.

In reviewing this film for its spiritual value, it is suggested that the viewer replay several key scenes as they are described here, which are particularly evocative.  In the beginning of the film, there are numerous allusions to British colonialism, the disparity between rich and poor which exists in Shanghai, and the search of a young boy for meaning in the context of "God."  It is notable that the parents are not helpful in giving their son any guidance as to his religious questions.  So he is left to ponder the difficult questions of life alone.  He tells his mother:  "Maybe God is our dream and we are his!"

Throughout the film, Jim moves back and forth between believing in a supreme being and not believing.  He declares himself an atheist, yet throughout the film, it is apparent that Jim wants to believe in God.  This question is especially notable in death scenes: with the doctor in the internment camp trying to revive the dead, with the young Japanese pilot who has been shot, and with Mrs. Victor (Miranda Richardson) who dies in the stadium.

The disparity between rich and poor disturbs Jim before the war. While his parents turn their heads from the poverty around them, he is troubled by the beggars and the masses of Chinese in the streets trying to escape from the advancing Japanese army.

Among the more informative themes underlying the text, the issue of good and evil is profoundly addressed through the juxtaposition of "enemies" and "allies." The British, American, Chinese and Japanese cultures are represented in the film. To look at the roles these national groups are assigned will provide important information.

The British are given roles of colonizer, wealthy investors, and in the internment camp, healer and educator as portrayed by the doctor. The Americans are assigned the roles of mercenaries, military pilots and saviors. The Chinese are assigned the roles of the exploited (slaves) or merchants. The Japanese are given the roles of invader, captor, kamikaze pilot and friend.

The "good" and "evil" elements of the characters and the societies they represent overlap, so that the humanity of the individual overrides the "cultural stereotype."  For example, the scene in which Jim shows respect for the Japanese pilots is extremely moving, and the transcendence of respect over fear is provocative.  The friendship that is woven between Jim and the Japanese youth who desires to be a kamikaze pilot is the most touching and revealing relationship in the film, for it models again the humanity of its characters rather than the roles they have been assigned by history.

The two boys, on opposite sides of the barbed wire fence which separates the internment camp from an airfield, become friends -- never a word spoken in common, only a smile and a vision shared.  They protect each other from harm, and Jim is overcome with grief when the boy is killed at the end of the film by one of the American mercenaries.  Jim tries to revive him, believing he can bring the "would-be" pilot back to life, but he fails.

The Japanese commander of the internment camp is at once cruel and brutal and intensely human.  Occasionally, the viewer is allowed to see his struggle and desire to be kind, but his role prevents him from it.

In the camp, Jim becomes the barterer and the rescuer.  He has learned from Basie to politically ingratiate himself in order to survive.  Jim takes upon himself the role of savior, as he desires to bring the dead back to life, or sacrifice himself to the Japanese commander to save the life of another.

Life and death are presented in constant tension in *Empire of the Sun*.  In many circumstances survival depends on the death of others, as in the holding camp, when the death of one individual means more food for another.  Death is always present as a threat; to live, characters must sometimes feign death as in the stadium scene.

In reviewing the scene at the stadium, where the symbols

of "opulence" have been gathered from the wealthy British homes and left in the sun for some future purpose, the interaction between Jim and Mrs. Victor is revealing.  She is dying, and Jim remains with her pretending to be dead, so that they will not have to continue on the forced march.  The next morning, Jim awakes and sees the woman lying very still.  There is a strange white light which moves across the sky and ripples across her body.  Jim's reaction is hopeful -- he thinks her soul is going up to heaven, again showing his ambivalence with regard to his belief in God. In reality, the light was the reflection of the bomb being dropped at Hiroshima.  Spielberg created a cinematic statement in this scene, where faith in life after death represented by the "light" is juxtaposed with the destruction of an atomic bomb.

One of the most important discoveries in the film involves Jim's rejection of Basie.  The viewer knows that Basie used Jim throughout the story, but the child could only see friendship. Jim's realization that Basie was not his friend, but a self-serving individual devoid of human compassion is dramatized when the young Japanese pilot is killed by one of Basie's mercenaries. In a touching scene, Jim tries to revive the boy as he had seen the doctor try to do with so many of the interned. Unable to bring his friend back to life and in the wake of Basie's racial slur against the young pilot, Jim rejects the man and with him the inhumane, exploitative elements of society.

It is suggested that *Empire of the Sun* be read prior to screening, as Spielberg took many liberties with the storyline, and both the autobiography and the film are valuable in their own portrayal of human conflict and the survival of human decency and hope in the midst of war.

*The Neverending Story* (1984) - UK/Germany - Fantasy

**Synopsis:**

A young boy named Bastian has just lost his mother. Unable to find comfort from his father, he turns to books where he can lose himself in his imagination.  One day Bastian visits a bookstore where he borrows an ornately-bound book called *The Neverending Story*.  Upon reading it, Bastian is pulled into a fantastic world inhabited by incredible creatures.

Fantasia, a kingdom which is ruled by a child-Empress, is being destroyed by the Nothing.  The young warrior Atreyu is the only "innocent" who can save the kingdom.  A true fantasy adventure for children, *The Neverending Story* is an interesting allegory and a remarkable parable about good and evil and personal integrity.

**Analysis:**

This fantasy takes a young boy named Atreyu through an amazing journey, testing his courage and character, pitting him against the forces of darkness.  His goal: to find a new name for the Empress and save her life.

Atreyu must pass through The Swamps of Sadness, the Sphinxes, and the Magic Mirror Gate to reach the Southern Oracle.  As he journeys he must evade the forces of evil, epitomized in the creature of darkness, the Gmork.  He loses his horse, Ortex, in the Swamp of Sadness, confronts his true self in the Magic Mirror Gate, and speaks to the Southern Oracle.  The Oracle informs Atreyu that only a human child can give the Empress a new name, and he can only find a human child beyond the boundaries of Fantasia.

It is at this point that Atreyu comes face to face with evil in the image of a wolf-like creature.  Gmork reveals the meaning of his journey and the reason for the destruction of Fantasia.  The creature also reveals to Atreyu that Fantasia has no boundaries. Atreyu defends himself against the creature and kills him.

Thinking he has failed in his quest, Atreyu locates the Empress and learns that the boy Bastian, who is reading the story, is the key to its resolution.

At its basic level, the film is a fantasy with interesting creatures and a typical cast of characters:  a ruler, a hero, a problem to be solved which will save the world.

It is a story within a story, and what makes it truly creative is that the human boy Bastian is pulled into the story itself and he must cooperate in order for the story to end well.  It is Bastian who must offer the Empress a new name, the name of his recently deceased mother.

**Issues of Spiritual Relevance:**

On a metaphorical level, the story is a warning to Bastian of what will happen if he leaves the world of imagination.  Bastian is not doing well in school, draws unicorns, and lives in the world of books.  His father tells him he has to stop running away from his problems and put his feet on the ground.

The destruction of Fantasia represents the destruction of the imagination.  Atreyu is "Bastian" who must be a warrior and fight against the destruction.  He must resist the sadness (Swamp of Sadness-reference to his mother's death), he must resist despair (the Nothing--the loss of hope and dreams), he must have confidence in himself (pass through the Sphinxes), and see himself as he really is (Move through the Magic Mirror Gate).

The ritual of giving the Empress a new name can be read psychologically as passing on the identity of his mother to another. Bastian thereby is able to let his mother's memory go by displacing her outside of himself, only to see her memory live on in his imagination.

The Gmork, who represents evil and confronts Atreyu with the philosophical underpinnings of the story, states that he is the representative of the power behind the Nothing.  He describes a conspiracy, where those without dreams and hope are easy to control, and that power resides within those who can then control the hopeless.

On a universal level, the story may be read as a warning to adults about the power of the imagination and creative side of life. *The Neverending Story* can also be read as a stern warning to society about the need for hope and dreams. Without them, any evil force may overtake the will of the people, as people without hope and those who have no dreams are easy to control. The social and political ramifications of such issues can also be addressed.

The film provides values which are constructive for children, and it encourages children to read and discover the world of books. However, some of the symbolism might be missed unless pointed out by parents. Young teens to young adults would benefit most from the spiritual meaning of the film.

*Shadowlands* (1993)  UK - Drama

**Synopsis:**

*Shadowlands* is based on the life of children's fantasy and spiritual writer, C.S. Lewis (portrayed by Sir Anthony Hopkins). A professor at Oxford University in 1952, Lewis is revered as a philosopher by the public for his spiritual writings and criticized by his colleagues for his interest in writing children's fantasy.

A confirmed bachelor who lives with his brother, Lewis meets an American woman, who is enchanted by his writing, and an unlikely friendship forms.  When the woman's marriage ends, she and her son move to England, where Lewis and his brother build a relationship with them.  Lewis and Joy (portrayed by Debra Winger) form a marriage of convenience so that she may stay in England.  She develops cancer, and his journey with her through her illness brings him into touch with the real meaning of love.

**Analysis/Issues of Spiritual Relevance:**

*Shadowlands* is a film about spirituality.  Based on a true story, it relates an incident in the life of C.S. Lewis, when he meets and marries an American woman who has remarkable insights into his character.

*Shadowlands* is about love and the pain which accompanies love.  The value of this film lies in the transformation of Lewis from theorist to realist.  His conversion is so inspiring and his redemption so believable that the viewer cannot be unaffected.  A man who has never experienced the meaning of love in emotional and physical terms, Lewis speaks of it esoterically in his classes and lectures with a smug indifference, insulating himself from emotions and maintaining himself in an intellectual milieu in which he pays no price.

Joy experiences all the emotions of life.  When she becomes ill, she suffers greatly.  There are notable scenes in which Lewis confronts himself in the midst of this tragedy, and the simple wisdom which results is inspiring.

Insights about prayer and the presence of God are also valuable for the viewer's reflection. In one scene, the minister and Lewis are having a brief conversation about the necessity of prayer in the face of adversity. Lewis states that he prays constantly -- not to ask God to save Joy's life -- but because he can do nothing else; he must in order to survive. "Prayer," he says, "does not change God, it changes me."

After Joy enters his world, Lewis begins to reach out to others, something he has not done before. She tells him that he has arranged a life in which he is either older or smarter than those around him. He is "on top" in every situation. Joy challenges his complacency and order, and Lewis begins to find an interest in one of his students who appears in need of help. Lewis discovers that the student's father is also a teacher, and he learns from the boy that "we read to know we are not alone."

Lewis is humbled by the circumstances of his new life, takes on the responsibility of Joy's son and is opened to learn from others.  His marriage of convenience becomes a marriage of true love and devotion, as he and his wife are remarried "before God" while Joy's cancer is in remission.

A moving film with intellectual, moral and spiritual levels which are enlightening, the viewer is challenged to reflect upon the reality Lewis intellectually understood and spoke of in his writings yet was unable to comprehend in himself until he met Joy Gresham.  Lewis recognized that due to the pain he experienced as a child after his mother's death, he had unconsciously barred himself from relationships so he would not have to endure the pain which accompanies love.  The metaphor for Lewis' behavior, which also can be found in his writings is simply stated:  "We all live in the shadowlands!"

---

*Age of Innocence* (1993) - US - Drama.

**Synopsis:**

The film is set in the 1870s in New York City among the aristocracy.  Newland Archer (Daniel Day Lewis) is engaged to marry May Welland (Winona Rider), a woman who anchors him to the traditions and conventions of Old New York society.  When he meets the Countess Olenska (Michelle Pfeiffer), a distant cousin who has returned to America to seek the comfort and acceptance of her family after a failed marriage, Archer is drawn to her intelligence and free-thinking style.  The story evolves around the activities of the tribe who conspire to keep the two potential lovers apart, without ever divulging their hidden agenda.

**Analysis:**

*Age of Innocence* is a film of great passion and beauty. The director has embellished his creation with a myriad of film techniques to bestow meaning upon his characters and the film's themes. With color, slow motion, the emptying of spaces, use of narration, dissolves and the extensive employment of motifs, Scorcese romanticizes his characters and their era, a world apart from the viewer's experience. Roger Ebert described the film vividly:

> *Age of Innocence represents a world completely alien to us. By the end we realize these people have all the same emotions, passions, fears and desires that we do. They value them more highly and are less careless with them and do not in the cause of self-indulgence choose a moment's pleasure over a lifetime's exquisite and romantic regret.*[9]

The characters in *Age of Innocence* care deeply about the repercussions of their actions. The viewer longs to see Newland and Ellen together because of their passionate love for each other. Yet Ellen must seek a divorce from her husband, who has been unfaithful to her, leaving her an outcast in New York Victorian society. So too, Newland must break his promise to marry May in order for such a union to be accomplished.

Newland and Ellen are ahead of their time in terms of their liberal view of relationships and values. Both see through the hypocrisy of their social conventions and wish to live above it. Both find the pain of their unconsummated love unbearable. Yet, in the midst of their temptation, their mutual sense of integrity and honor do not allow them to abandon the rules of the tribe in order to pursue a life together.

It is May who actually seals the fate of the aspiring lovers when she tells Ellen, who is her cousin, that she is to have a child. The expected progeny cements the passionless but civilized marriage between Newland and May, and leaves Ellen and Newland forever estranged.

**Issues of Spiritual Relevance:**

Issues which are discussed in the film include honor, commitment, romantic and spiritual love.  Through the struggles of the characters, the viewer is drawn into their world of love and temptation, and an appreciation of spiritual love which grew over time between Newland and May.

As Newland reflects on his life after his wife's death, he recognizes the goodness and ultimate gift he has received through the life he shared with May and their children.  Now free to seek out Ellen and encouraged by his son to do so, he is unable to face her, having truly become the man whose life he lived.

The personal sacrifice both characters endured for the welfare of others is touching and a powerful model for a 1990s audience in its examination of moral courage.

_Searching for Bobby Fischer_  (1993) - US - Drama

**Synopsis:**

_Searching for Bobby Fischer_ tells the story of chess protege, Josh Waitzkin, who discovers a talent for chess while watching speed chess being played in the park in New York City. His father, a sports writer, recognizing his son's gift, enlists the expertise of a chess mentor. Josh enters the world of competitive chess, which challenges his goodness and his relationship with his father. The wisdom of his mother and Josh's own integrity endure through the ambition-driven milieu in which he finds himself entrenched.

**Analysis:**

This film is based on the life of Josh Waitzkin, a chess protege, whom many believed had the talent of Bobby Fischer. The story takes the viewer into the Waitzkin family and exposes the inner workings of the chess world, its competitions and its obsession with "being the best." The genius with which Josh has been invested and the two worlds from which he draws his lessons in the playing of the game converge to propel this heart-warming film to its inspiring conclusion.

Through the love and sensitivity of his mother, the drive and ambition of his father, the selfish abandon of his professional chess mentor, and the friendship and savvy of his street-wise chess partner, Josh becomes a champion with a heart of gold. For Josh, chess is a gift, something which he enjoys as much as baseball or camping and fishing with his father. For the others in the competitive world, chess is their entire reason for living. It is Josh who provides the adults with the perspective they lack, when in a championship tournament he gives his opponent the opportunity to call a draw when he realizes that his opponent is beaten. Lacking Josh's instinct and ability to analyze the board many moves ahead, Josh's opponent is unable to recognize the impending loss. Since he has been taught only to win, the boy impending loss. Since he has been taught only to win, the boy refuses the draw and loses the game.

Josh's generosity and sense of humanity are touching and redeeming, as he blends his kindness with the art of chess, i.e., knowing when to play the opponent and when to use the tactics of analysis in playing only the board.

## Issues of Spiritual Relevance:

In our competitive society, many values become lost to our children in the pursuit of winning. Here is a film which portrays a young boy whose inner concern for others does not allow him be altered by his genius even at the risk of disapproving adults.

Lies, deceit and the dehumanizing of one's opponent are traits encouraged by Josh's chess mentor as a means of motivating Josh to learn the tactics of chess and the psychological preparation necessary to sustain the win. Bobby Fischer, whom Josh's talent mirrors, was known to show contempt for his opponents. But Josh is able to resist both the ambitions and cruelty of his mentor and the sometimes misguided enthusiasm of his sports writer father.

Balance, friendship, generosity and love of the game for its own sake are values which emerge from this fine film which is recommended for all ages.


*Nobody's Fool*  (1994) - US - Drama

**Synopsis:**

New Bath, New York is the setting for this warm-hearted examination of an aging construction worker living in a blue-collar community.  Paul Newman plays the title role of Sully with a crusty independence and sassy sense of humor that endears him to the audience.

The central theme in the film deals with Sully's relationship with his son, a college instructor, who has a rocky marriage and two children of his own.  Having been literally abandoned by his father as a child, the son is bitter, and the film discusses the lost years of fatherhood and Sully's attempt to become both father and grandfather to Michael and his son.

**Analysis:**

*Nobody's Fool* is a film about relationships, but it is also concerned with the appearance of reality. On a superficial level Sully is not well-appreciated by the members of the community. However, as the story unfolds, the viewer becomes aware that his presence is pivotal to the cohesion of the community and the relationships of its members. Appearing to have made nothing of himself and his life, he is branded a failure, yet no member of the community is untouched by him nor able to function completely without him. This fact is dramatized by his being released from jail in order to serve as a pall-bearer for a funeral.

*Nobody's Fool* is also a film about loss and forgiveness and the effects of an absent father on the lives of his children.

**Issues of Spiritual Relevance:**

*Nobody's Fool* is especially relevant to the spiritual enlightenment of its viewers.  It addresses family responsibility and commitment to children and their rearing and exposes the emotional scars children of absent fathers retain throughout their lives.  The film also brings its viewers into touch with their sense of community, i.e., their place in the lives of others.  Sully was important to many individuals within his small town in upstate New York: his landlord, his friend and fellow laborer, his attorney, his boss, his boss' wife, and the woman with Alzheimer's.  He gave to others the way he had never learned to care for his son, and his sense of obligation is notable in his dealings with the other characters.

The viewer might also give special attention to Sully's relationship to his own father, an alcoholic and wife abuser, and the memories that haunted him each time he entered the abandoned family home.

The film is a powerful story of family ties and responsibilities and the way in which forgiveness and redemption work together to bring peace to previously estranged individuals.

*Dead Man Walking* (1995) - US - Prison drama

**Synopsis:**

*Dead Man Walking* tells the true story of Sister Helen Prejean's (Susan Sarandon) relationship with a condemned murderer, Matthew Poncelet (Sean Penn), sentenced to be executed by lethal injection.  In search of a retrial, the convicted killer seeks out someone to serve as a mediator.  Sr. Prejean, a nun who lives and works in the projects in Louisiana, is approached by a mutual contact.  After visiting the convict, she finds herself drawn into a legal, then spiritual relationship with the man.

The families of the victims, the public and the convicted murderer's family all enter into relationships with the nun, as she becomes Matthew Poncelet's spiritual advisor.

## Analysis:

The film is powerful and honest in its portrayal of its characters and their inner and interpersonal conflicts. All sides of the controversy over the death penalty are presented as Sr. Helen interacts with the individuals whose lives have been touched by the crime.

The redemption of the criminal is Sr. Helen's focus, and she works at bringing a sense of God's love to him as he approaches his own death. The criminal denies his culpability in the crimes and remains without remorse until the end of the film.

The final scenes of *Dead Man Walking* are powerful and illuminating. The performances of Sean Penn as the man on death row and Susan Sarandon as his spiritual director are unforgettable.

## Issues of Spiritual Relevance:

*Dead Man Walking*, on a literal level, is a film about the justification of the death penalty. Whatever the viewer's point of view on this controversial issue, one leave's the film with a broadened perspective.

As a representative of Jesus on earth, Sr. Helen is committed to her ministry to work among the poor and those most despised by society.  She finds herself drawn into a world of crime and criminal behavior of which she has no knowledge or experience.  Yet her ministry prevents her from abandoning this man, when his soul is in ultimate danger of eternal condemnation. Scorned by those who see her as a traitor to the victims, and judged harshly by her family and the families of the victims, Sr. Helen bravely perseveres in her commitment to Christian love.

She begs Poncelet to pray, to read the Bible, and to seek forgiveness for his part in the crimes.  She repeatedly tells him that Jesus loves him.  As his death approaches, he loses his macho facade and breaks his resolve to cover his own responsibility for the crimes and confesses to the nun.  In that moment -- the moment of his redemption -- he is free.

As Poncelet goes to the death chamber, he stands strapped to the executioner's table, facing the parents of the victims and asks their forgiveness.  Then, fixed on the face of Sr. Helen -- the face of love -- he succumbs to the lethal drugs.

A call to social action and a gift of enormous spiritual magnitude, *Dead Man Walking* is a critical film for the 90s, offering a society poor in spiritual light both hope and salvation. Sr. Helen Prejean is a woman of courage and unwavering commitment to follow the example of Jesus, an extraordinary role model for everyone who has been touched by her story.

# 5

# USING FILM AS A TEACHING TOOL

The preceding chapters have discussed the ways in which individuals can address their film experiences in order to elicit the spiritual elements which can motivate and inspire them. With an increase in visual literacy and an awareness of the techniques used by filmmakers to bring meaning to their work, the parent or teacher is outfitted for facilitating the discussion of film and its spiritual dimension in a group setting.

This chapter will offer a few basic suggestions as to how the parent or teacher may approach this facilitation.

## IN AN EDUCATIONAL SETTING

The classroom or Sunday School session, youth group, or retreat all provide opportunities for values education and the discussion of issues of a spiritual and moral nature.

Your curriculum or program begins with a value or moral principle which you wish to impart to or explore with the group. No matter what the age and maturity level of the individuals involved, the facilitator will be able to use a film or portion of a film to demonstrate the point of the exercise or theme for the session.

For example, if the facilitator wishes to teach the group about the meaning of respect for others within a competitive setting, screening *Searching for Bobby Fischer* might be appropriate. The participants can watch the conflicts of the characters as they struggle with their human failings and be inspired by the unselfish concern of the protagonist for the good of others. The balance that is struck in this fine film will teach the participants constructive thinking in terms of ambition, talent and reward within the parameters of their own religious and moral code.

A suggested format might include the following:

1.      Introduce the topic to the group.

2.      Provide a list of sample questions for discussion which you

        instruct the students to read, then save until after the film

        is screened.

3.      Screen the film.

4.      Depending on the age of the participants, use a group

        discussion or break the larger group into smaller groups to

        discuss specific questions listed on the handout.

5.      Integrate the learning experience with the whole group and

        summarize.


General questions which can be listed on the handout

should cover the individual's personal response to the picture and

questions which lead into the heart of the value you wish to

explore:

1.      Why did you like or dislike the film?

2.      Which characters did you like and why?

3.     What important lessons are there in the film?

4.     How did the film make you feel?

5.     What was special about Josh and the way he treated his opponents?

6.     What did his teacher say or do that hurt or helped Josh?

7.     What did his father say or do that hurt or helped Josh?

8.     What did his mother say or do that hurt or helped Josh?

9.     Is winning important?  Is doing your best important?

10.    What type of person would you be in this situation?

11.    Are there positive role models in the film? If so, who are they and why?

Of course, the format and questions listed above are guidelines and must be adapted to the age level of the group. More sophisticated questions would be used in an adult discussion group, and a simpler approach would be necessary for younger children.

For teachers who would like to use film more wisely in the elementary, junior high, or high school setting, there is a wonderful book available for integrating visual images into instruction. I highly recommend *Visual Messages: Integrating Imagery into Instruction* by David Considine and Gail Haley. Their book offers examples of films to be used in teaching most subjects at various levels, as well as approaches to integrating the film messages into the context of the topic to be explored.

## CLERGY

Clergy who are in touch with the social and spiritual dynamics of film may find the opportunity to integrate the mention of a film experience in their sermons or counseling sessions. Since the majority of individuals in society are visual learners, motion pictures can be useful in helping individuals comprehend their own circumstances more clearly through identification with film characters and their struggles to come to moral decisions. In this way, carefully selected films can serve to reinforce one's counseling and prayerful discernment.

Examples of films which might be useful in this arena depending upon the needs of the viewer could include: *Gandhi* for an experience in moral courage and integrity; *Dead Man Walking* for the experience of commitment to Christian love in the face of opposition; *Ordinary People* for a discussion of guilt and responsibility and the integrity of family relationships; *When A Man Loves A Woman* for a discussion of alcoholism and its effects on the family and the struggle for personal dignity, redemption and healing; *Avalon* for a discussion of the American values which lead to the disintegration of the family.

# 6

# CONCLUSION

The world of film has many sides, and it is our good fortune that we have discovered the spiritual dimensions of this cultural artifact and popular American pastime in light of its relationship to art.

As visual parables, motion pictures bring the audience into touch with humanity and the complexity of inner as well as interpersonal conflicts. Films suggest ways in which viewers can become better Christians, better neighbors, better friends, better citizens. They take their audiences through pain and disappointment, soul-wrenching turmoil and alienation to a better place of hope and redemption.

Many of the film characters discussed in the previous chapter give the reader reason to care, to pray and to act. Others reinforce a belief in the essential goodness of the human heart and serve as role models. Just as film characters and their circumstances reflect real issues and real social dilemmas, so too does film as visual parable ask its audience to understand and perhaps even change that reality.

# ENDNOTES


1.  Center for Media and Values literature, Los Angeles.

2.  David M. Considine and Gail E. Haley, *Visual Messages: Integrating Imagery Into Instruction*, (Englewood Colorado: Teacher Ideas Press, 1992), 12.

3.  Louis Giannetti, *Understanding Movies* (Englewood Cliffs, N.J: Prentice Hall, 1976) 48.

4.  *Visual Messages* 167.

5.  Janet Meyer, *A Humanistic Analysis of the Films of Sydney Pollack*, Masters thesis, 1992.

6.  Kurt Luedtke, *Out of Africa*, screenplay, 1985.

7.  Vincent Canby, "Screen: *Out of Africa*: Starring Meryl Streep," *New York Times* 18 Dec 1985: 25.

8.  M. Scott Peck, M.D. *The Road Less Traveled* (New York: Simon and Schuster, 1978), 168.

9.  Roger Ebert review, *Age of Innocence, Cinemania 95*. CD-Rom.

# APPENDICES

# APPENDIX A

## GLOSSARY

Composition
: The placement of people or objects within the frame.

Congruence
: A technique in which image and sound support each other.

Counterpoint
: A technique in which image is placed in opposition to sound to make a statement.

Cut
: An individual strip of film consisting of a single shot; the separation of two pieces of action as a transition; a verb meaning to join shots together in the editing process; an order to end a take.

Escapism
: The psychological process whereby the viewer leaves the real world and enjoys the film for its entertainment value.

Fish-eye Lens
: An extreme wide-angle lens which distorts the image. Creates a sense of psychological imbalance, drunkenness, confusion.

Frame
: A single photographic image imprinted on a length of film.

Genre
: A group of stories which contain similar character types, props, themes, locations,

settings and eras.   A formula motion picture.   Examples include the western, adventure film, film noir, drama, horror, science fiction, romance, fantasy, comedy.

High Angle Shot    A technique in which the camera points downward at an object or person in order to imply something.   For example, in American conventions, such an angle implies subjugation or insignificance.

Identification    The psychological process whereby the viewer recognizes similar traits between himself and the character(s) or experiences described in the plot causing him to buy in to the storyline.

Juxtaposition    A technique whereby the filmmaker edits dissimilar shots next to each other in order to make a statement.

Location    A place outside the studio where shooting occurs.

Low Angle Shot    A technique in which the camera points upward at an object or person in order to imply something.   For example, in American conventions, such an angle implies power or dominance.

Media Literacy    The ability to read and interpret messages created by all forms of media.

| | |
|---|---|
| Mise-en-scene | A French term borrowed from the theatre which refers to the composition of visual elements within the frame. |
| Motif | A literary device used by filmmakers to emphasize a theme.  The motif is a repetition of an object, sound, or symbol. |
| Objective camera | The attempt to suggest that the camera acts as a passive recorder of what happens in front of it.  The use of objective camera relies on de-emphasis of technique, involving minimal camera movement and editing. |
| Scene | A structural unit of film, composed of one or more shots. |
| Script | A written description of the action, dialogue, and camera placement for a film. |
| Sequence | A structural unit of film using time, location or some pattern to link together a number of scenes. |
| Shot | A single, uninterrupted action of a camera. |
| Subjective camera | Shots simulating what a character actually sees.  May involve the use of distortion to create abnormal mental states. |

Take

A single uninterrupted action of a camera as seen by a filmmaker. It differs from a shot in that it refers to the unedited footage, while a shot is the uninterrupted action left after editing.

Vindication

The psychological process whereby the viewer buys into the storyline as a way of working through anger, hostility or a personal need to see justice served.

Wish Fulfillment

The psychological process whereby the viewer is drawn into the storyline because the circumstances of the story fulfill a need in her own life.

Visual Literacy

The ability to read and interpret images created by visual media such as film, television, advertising, news and magazine print.

# APPENDIX B

**RECOMMENDED FILMS**
**By Category**

*Denotes suitable for children under 12
**Mature themes. Parental guidance advised.

## INSPIRATIONAL: BIOGRAPHICAL

*An Angel At My Table*** 1991  MPAA Rating: R.  New Zealand.
Subject: The autobiography of New Zealand novelist and poet, Janet Frame, mistakenly diagnosed as a schizophrenic and hospitalized for many years.

*Gandhi* 1982  No Rating. India-UK.
Subject: The life and influence of Indian pacifist Mahatma Gandhi.

*Mask* 1985  MPAA Rating: PG-13
Subject: The life and relationships of a teenage boy whose disfiguring disease costs him his life.

*Not Without My Daughter*** 1991  MPAA Rating: PG-13
Subject: The imprisonment and escape of American Betty Mahmoody and her daughter from Iran. Several scenes of spousal abuse require caution by parents.

*Romero* 1989  MPAA Rating: PG-13
Subject: Biography of Archbishop Romero of El Salvador.

---

## INSPIRATIONAL: HISTORICAL

*Cool Runnings** 1993  MPAA Rating: PG
Subject: In the face of unbelievable odds, a Jamaican bobsled team competes in the Olympics.

*Empire of the Sun* 1987  MPAA Rating: PG
Subject: World War II in Shanghai and imprisonment of a young British boy.  Violence and death are strong themes. Good fare for teens and above.

*Glory* 1989  MPAA Rating: R
Subject: The civil war and the first Black regiment trained to fight for the North.  War violence and a whipping might be objectionable for younger viewers.

*Mission, The*** 1986  MPAA Rating: R
Subject: Jesuit missionaries in South America.  Violence.

*Year of Living Dangerously, The* 1983  MPAA Rating: PG
Subject: An American journalist in Indonesia during the dictatorship of Sukarno. Depiction of poverty and violence too intense for young viewers.

## INSPIRATIONAL: GENERAL

*Dave* 1993  MPAA Rating: PG-13
Subject: A man who looks like the president is recruited to serve in his place while the real executive is seriously ill and finds opportunities to improve the way in which social services are rendered to those in need.

*Phenomenon* 1996 MPAA Rating: PG-13
Subject: A man develops incredible knowledge and insights and believes he has been touched by a cosmic force. No sex, violence or objectionable language.


## CENTRAL THEME:
## CIVIL RIGHTS/DISCRIMINATION/RACISM

*Betrayed*** 1988  MPAA Rating: R
Subject: White supremacists in the Midwest. Themes include racism, murder, political assassination. Violence, language, sexual situations and white supremacist activity.

*Ghosts of Mississippi*** 1996  MPAA Rating: R
Subject: Racism in the South and the killing of Medgar Evers. Violent depiction of the murder and racist propaganda.

*Long Walk Home, The* 1990  MPAA Rating: PG
Subject: Civil rights issues.

*Mississippi Burning*** 1988  MPAA Rating: R
Subject: Racism in Mississippi as a backdrop to the disappearance of three civil rights workers. Themes include violence, racism, one scene of abuse against a woman, white supremacist propaganda.

*Philadelphia* 1993  MPAA Rating: PG-13
Subject: Illegal firing of a man with AIDS.  Themes include discrimination, gay rights issues/AIDS. Mild discussion of sexual themes and depiction of physical illness. No graphic sexual activity, nudity or violence.  Good for teens.

---

*Thunderheart* 1992  MPAA Rating: R
Subject: Native American issues on the Pine Ridge Reservation when FBI agents investigate a murder.  Graphic violence.

## CENTRAL THEME: COURAGE

*Lost in Yonkers* 1993  MPAA Rating: PG
Subject: A slow woman who lives with her mother is visited by her two young male cousins, who give her the courage to live life on her own.

*Of Mice and Men* 1939, 1981, 1992  MPAA Rating: PG-13
Subject: John Steinbeck's novel is brought to life about a man and his ward, who is retarded, and their struggle to survive in a hostile world.

*Rudy* 1993  MPAA Rating: PG
Subject: The dream of a young boy to play football for the University of Notre Dame is realized.

*Secret Garden, The** 1993  MPAA Rating: G
Subject: The adventures of an orphan who goes to live with her elusive uncle in England only to discover the secrets of the household and the enchantments of a secret garden.

## CENTRAL THEME: GOOD VERSUS EVIL

*Ladyhawke* 1985  MPAA Rating: PG-13
Subject: The mystical struggle between good and evil during the Inquisition and a love affair corrupted by an evil Bishop. Violence including hangings is a strong theme.

*Star Wars** 1977  MPAA Rating: PG
Subject: The classic story of the battle between good and evil in space.

*To Sleep With Anger* 1990  MPAA Rating: PG
Subject: Truth and deception. An old friend comes to visit a family and corrupts the lives of those with whom he comes in contact. A fine discussion of familial relationships and the personification of evil.

## CENTRAL THEME: MORAL DILEMMA

*A Few Good Men* 1992  MPAA Rating: R
Subject: An investigation of a murder of a marine at Guantanamo Bay and the illegal activities of the base commander who operates under the guise of honor and patriotism.

*Absence of Malice* 1981  MPAA Rating: PG-13
Subject: Journalism. No graphic sex, violence, nudity or language. Suicide and abortion are handled delicately. Younger viewers may not be able to follow storyline.

*Age of Innocence* 1993  MPAA Rating: PG
Subject: Illicit love. Themes include sexual temptation, social conventions which are explored but never violated. Exquisite filmmaking. No sex, violence, nudity or objectionable language.

*Aladdin* 1992 MPAA Rating: G
Subject: Animated tale set in the middle East which explores the principles of honesty, integrity, freedom and generosity.  No sex, violence, nudity or objectionable language.

*All the President's Men* 1976  MPAA Rating: PG
Subject: Watergate. No graphic sex, violence, nudity or objectionable language. Younger viewers may not be able to follow complexity of storyline.

*Amadeus* 1984  MPAA Rating: PG
Subject: The life of Mozart and his rival Salieri. Religious themes and the willful destruction of another human being and its moral consequences. Some crude language, depiction of the insane, death and alcoholism may be too intense for younger viewers. A lot of opera, but an outstanding film.

*American Anthem** 1986  MPAA Rating: PG-13
Subject: Amateur Sports.

*And Justice for All* 1979  MPAA Rating: R
Subject: The law and the buying and selling of justice.

*Arthur* 1981  MPAA Rating: PG
Subject: Wealth and responsibility. Prostitution and alcoholism are depicted. No graphic sex scenes or nudity. A couple of crude sexually-related anatomical references. A sad exploration of an alcoholic's search for meaning and love.

*Carlitos Way*** 1993  MPAA Rating: R
Subject: Drug dealing. Very mature themes involving drugs, sex and violence. Artistic depiction of a man who wants to change his life and those who will not allow him to leave the world of drug dealing. Parents should preview film before showing it to children, as the violence is brutal and very graphic. Language is also strong, as are sexual themes. Film techniques and camera angles are unique in their attempt to capture the interior psyche.

*Chariots of Fire* 1981  MPAA Rating: PG
Subject: The motives and problems of two athletes who run in the 1924 Olympics; one who must choose between honor and commitment to run for his country or observe his religious beliefs and not run on a holyday.

*City Hall* 1995  MPAA Rating: R
Subject: New York City politics.  Themes include mob activity, corruption and suicide.  Some objectionable language.

*Courage Under Fire* 1996  MPAA Rating: R
Subject: Investigation of courage and honor of a female helicopter pilot during Desert Storm. War violence, drugs, alcohol. Good for teens.

*Crazy People* 1990 MPAA Rating: R
Subject: Truth in advertising.

*The Crucible* 1996  MPAA Rating: R
Subject: The hysteria associated with the unjust condemnation of innocent people as witches in Salem, Massachusetts.

*Dances With Wolves* 1990  MPAA Rating: PG-13
Subject: Indian/White relations in the Sioux territory. Themes include graphic war violence, graphic depiction of animal desecration and hunting rituals, sexual activity, nudity.

*Death and the Maiden*** MPAA Rating: R
Subject: Political torture. Themes include rape and revenge.

*Extreme Measures* 1996. MPAA Rating: R.
Subject: Human experimentation for the purpose of medical advancement.  Two dilemmas are notable: choosing to save one

person over another in a crisis; using humans for experimental purposes without their consent. Objectionable language, violence, and graphic medical procedures. Parents should preview. Excellent medical ethics discussions should arise from viewing this picture.

*Fern Gully: The Last Rain Forest** 1992  MPAA Rating: G
Subject: Moral animated feature discussing the destruction of the rain forest.

*The Firm* 1993  MPAA Rating: R
Subject: Legal corruption. Themes include sex, violence and the mob. Some objectionable language in the form of expletives. Sexual situations and language.

*Fisher King, The*** 1991  MPAA Rating: R
Subject: A radio personality through his bigotry causes the death of a group of people in a restaurant, and fate helps him redeem himself by helping the husband of a woman who was killed. Full male nudity, sexual situations and language.  Violence. Psychological hallucinations presented in a way which might be frightening to children.  Parents should preview.

*Fried Green Tomatoes* 1991  MPAA Rating: PG-13
Subject: The story of a family's loves and losses in a rural Alabama settlement.  Themes include racism, domestic violence against women, Southern women's search for identity, compassion for the poor and homeless, friendship and loyalty, marital and inter-female relationships.  Some mature themes, including Klan violence, a domestic attack.  Female anatomical and physiological references.  Parents advised to screen prior to showing to younger children.

*Glengarry Glen Ross* 1992  MPAA Rating: R
Subject: The moral destruction of a group of real estate agents who cannot sell land and find themselves faced with the loss of their jobs.  Continuous objectionable language in the form of expletives.  A powerful film, despite the language, if it can be tolerated.  For older teens and adults.

*Good Son, The* 1993  MPAA Rating: R
Subject: A boy is sent to live with his relatives and becomes the object of his cousin's evil ways.  The moral dilemma focuses on the aunt's decision as to which boy to save.

*House of Games* 1987  MPAA Rating: R
Subject: Congames and addictive behavior. Themes include sex, gambling, psychological manipulation, murder.  Good for mature teens with guidance.

*Flatliners* 1990  MPAA Rating: R
Subject: A group of medical students experiment with life and death subjecting themselves to voluntary death, expecting to be resuscitated.

*Indecent Proposal*** 1993  MPAA Rating: R
Subject: prostitution and adultery. Themes are very mature though glossed over for palatability; sexual activity. Good for mature teens with guidance.

*In the Name of the Father* 1993  MPAA Rating: R
Subject: Political upheaval in Ireland between the Catholic and Protestant factions. Violence.

---

*Inherit the Wind** 1960, 1988  MPAA Rating: PG
Subject: The famous Scopes "monkey trial" which delves into the conflict between science and Scripture with regard to human origins.  Emphasis is freedom of religious belief and expression.

*Jeremiah Johnson* 1972  MPAA Rating: PG
Subject: The spiritual journey of a deserter in the 19th century. Violence, while not gratuitous, is a strong theme.

*Jurassic Park* 1993  MPAA Rating: PG-13
Subject: Genetic engineering. Violence which may be extremely frightening to younger viewers, as it is generated by prehistoric animals.

*Losing Isaiah*** 1995  MPAA Rating: R
Subject: Adoption. Themes include motherly love and race with regard to adoption policies.

*Night Falls on Manhattan*** 1997 MPAA Rating: R
Subject: New York City police corruption and the meaning of justice.  Violence and language give this film its R rating.
A powerful examination of how to achieve justice within the boundaries of the legal system.

*Rebel Without A Cause* 1955  No Rating
Subject: Post World War II drama depicting the fragmentation of the American family and juvenile delinquency in middle class white families.

*Regarding Henry* 1991   MPAA Rating: PG-13
Subject:  A tragic accident brings a couple back together who have been estranged, re-establishing their love for each other.

*School Ties* 1992  MPAA Rating: PG-13
Subject: Anti-semitism and honor in a parochial boarding school.

*Searching for Bobby Fischer** See Filmography.

*Schindlers List*** 1993  MPAA Rating: R
Subject: The Holocaust. Themes include anti-semitism, genocide. Graphic depiction of death camps, gas chambers, extensive nudity, some sexual activity.  Good for mature teens due to its historic relevance.

*Slingblade*** 1996  MPAA Rating: R
Subject: Justification of murder. Mature themes involve verbal and psychological abuse, murder, mental illness, retardation.  No graphic sex or nudity. Language is graphic in terms of descriptions of murders; crude and violence-inducing with regard to a particular family relationship, but limited.  Exceptional filmmaking with the examination of the moral dilemma involving premeditated murder for the purpose of protecting loved ones.  Parents advised to screen prior to showing to children.

*Swing Kids* 1993  MPAA Rating: PG-13
Subject: Teen resistance to the Nazis in Germany.  Themes include violence, anti-semitism, Nazi indoctrination of youth, swing dancing.  Good for teens.

*They Shoot Horses, Don't They?*** 1969  MPAA Rating: PG
Subject: Marathon exploitation in 1920s.  Themes include suicide, murder, despair, exploitation.

*Wall Street* 1987  MPAA Rating: R.
Subject: Corruption of a stock broker by a megalomaniac whose account he wants. Themes include inside trading, greed,

ruthlessness in the pursuit of power. Difficult to follow at times. Recommended for older teens and up. Language and sexuality. Some female nudity.

*When A Man Loves A Woman*** 1994  MPAA Rating: R
Subject: An alcoholic woman struggles to survive as a person, mother and wife.  Excellent portrayal of the issues involved in co-dependency and recovery.  Parents should preview.

*With Honors* 1994  MPAA Rating: PG-13
Subject: Individual's relationship with the government; homelessness and social responsibility; the true meaning of honor. Mild language with some sexual overtones.


## CENTRAL THEME: OVERCOMING ADVERSITY

*La Familia* 1995 MPAA Rating: R
Subject: Mexican-American family struggling to survive in a Los Angeles barrio.

*Lean on Me** 1989  MPAA Rating: PG-13
Subject: High school minorities. Inspiring look at a dedicated principal and his minority students who are socialized to fail within the system.  Themes include high school pregnancy, dysfunctional families, drug use.  All themes are handled with sensitivity. Excellent film for age twelve and above.  Younger children should have guidance.

*Man Without A Face* 1993  MPAA Rating: PG-13
Subject: The social alienation of a teacher who is facially deformed.

*Stand and Deliver** 1987  MPAA Rating: PG
Subject: High school minorities. Themes include the relationship between a high school teacher and his students and his dedication to bringing them into the mainstream educational pipeline through their success in mathematics.  Some language.

## CENTRAL THEME: REDEMPTION

*A Christmas Carol** 1938, 1951, 1984  MPAA Rating: G
Subject: Charles Dickens tale of poverty and generosity.

*City of Joy*** 1992  MPAA Rating: PG-13
Subject: Poverty in India. Parents should preview.

*Dead Man Walking*** See Filmography.

*Defending Your Life* 1991  MPAA Rating: PG
Subject: The review of an individual's deeds on earth before a panel in heaven.

*Groundhog Day* 1993  MPAA Rating: PG
Subject: A weather man is caught up in a metaphysical plot which forces him to repeat the same day until he is able to show the love and respect for others necessary to redeem himself.

*Hoosiers* 1986  MPAA Rating: PG
Subject: An ex-college basketball coach is given one last chance to prove himself when he is hired to coach an Indiana high school basketball team.  Themes include rural versus city living and values, father-son relationships, alcoholism and recovery, discipline and team-work.  Excellent film for children 12 and above.

*Preacher's Wife, The* 1996 MPAA Rating: PG
Subject: A Baptist minister begins to lose hope and faith which affects his family life, and an angel is sent down to save the marriage and the community.  Best scenes are played out by the son; viewers may find inspiration in the simple dilemmas discussed in this sincere but weak film.  Good for families but prepare for an abundance of singing from Whitney Houston.

*Renaissance Man* 1994  MPAA Rating: PG-13
Subject: A man at a dead end in his career is hired to teach army recruits basic reading.

*Shawshank Redemption, The*** 1995  MPAA Rating: R
Subject: The effects of imprisonment on the prisoners and their ability to survive on the outside; the imprisonment of an innocent man. Themes include beatings, one graphic sexual encounter (heterosexual), gang rape in prison, nudity, crude language, suicide, hope and redemption. Parents advised to screen prior to showing to children due to brutality.

*Spitfire Grill, The* 1996  MPAA Rating: PG-13
Subject: The rehabilitation of a female convict as she begins life anew in a small New England town.  Themes of redemption, trust, suspicion, and the destructiveness of detraction and fear are beautifully enacted.


## CENTRAL THEME: RELATIONSHIPS

*84 Charing Cross Road* 1987  MPAA Rating: PG
Subject: The love affair between two individuals who carry on a relationship through their letters.

*A River Runs Through It* 1992  MPAA Rating: PG
Subject: Family communication, art and religion in a Montana setting. Some violence.

*Avalon** 1990  MPAA Rating: PG
Subject: The breakdown of the immigrant family in America. Excellent filmmaking.

*A Walk in the Clouds** 1995 MPAA Rating: PG-13
Subject: Family and responsibility.  Pregnancy out of wedlock is a theme.

*Babe** 1995  MPAA Rating: G
Subject: An allegory about love and relationships as seen through the animal kingdom.  Good for exploration of differences among groups.

*Cadence* 1993  MPAA Rating: PG-13
Subject: Bigotry, honor and respect among white and black soldiers in prison.  Some violence and language.

*Color Purple, The* 1985  MPAA Rating: PG-13
Subject: Life of black women in the south. Sexual activity, incest, lesbian overtones and abuse are strong themes. Guidance recommended for younger viewers.

*Death of a Salesman* 1951, 1985   No Rating
Subject: The relationship of a salesman to his work and his family. Alienation is a theme.

*Driving Miss Daisy* 1989 MPAA Rating: PG
Subject: Gender, age and ethnic relations in a household in Georgia.

*Edward Scissorhands** 1990  MPAA Rating: PG-13
Subject: A fantasy about a boy who is invented by a scientist with scissors in place of his hands and how he interacts with the members of the community.  The focus is on the beauty of being different, as his scissors allow him to create art but prevent him from touching another human being and experiencing love.

*Forrest Gump* 1995  MPAA Rating: PG-13
Subject: A retarded man lives a life of innocence and love. War violence, amputation, sexuality, and drug abuse are themes which might be objectionable for younger viewers.

*The Glass Menagerie* 1950, 1973, 1987  MPAA Rating: PG
Subject: Tennessee Williams story about the illusions and desperation of a family during the depression. No sex, violence, nudity or objectionable language.  Highly lyrical in its dialogue.

*Home Alone* 1990  MPAA Rating: PG
Subject: A young boy is left home when his family goes to Europe and discovers how important they are to him.  Theme of reconciliation of family members is the principal focus.

*Heaven and Earth*  1993  MPAA Rating: R
Subject: A Vietnam veteran loves and marries a Vietnamese woman and brings her to the United States.  Sexual and violent themes would restrict this to older teens and above.

*Joy Luck Club* 1993  MPAA Rating: R
Subject: The lives of three Chinese-American women and their relationships with their daughters. A comparison of cultures between China and America.

*Like Water for Chocolate*** 1992  MPAA Rating: R. Mexico.
Subject: A magical-romantic and very unusual story about love, sensuality, and cooking. Mature themes. Parents should preview.

*Marvin's Room* 1996  MPAA Rating: PG-13
Subject: Family relationships and unconditional love.

*Mr. Hollands Opus** 1996  MPAA Rating: PG
Subject: A music teacher's influence on his students; parent-child relationships.  Some profanity; adult themes.

*Memories of Me* 1988  MPAA Rating: PG-13
Subject: The relationship between an estranged father and son.

*Michael* 1996 MPAA Rating: PG-13
Subject: An angel visits earth in order to bring two people together. Film should be previewed by parents due to the nature of the moral code of the angel.  This liberal view may offend some viewers.

*Lion King, The** 1994  MPAA Rating: G
Subject: An animated tale of status and role differentiation within the animal kingdom. An allegory.

*Mrs. Doubtfire* 1993  MPAA Rating: PG-13
Subject: Family responsibility and communication.

*Ordinary People*** 1980  MPAA Rating: R
Subject: The dynamics of interpersonal relationships in a family devastated by the death of the older son.  Discussion of suicide and one scene involving crude sexual references; otherwise an excellent film from an artistic as well as psychological viewpoint. Too intense for younger viewers.

*Out of Africa* 1985. See Filmography.

*Places in the Heart* 1984  MPAA Rating: PG
Subject: The struggle of three isolated and alienated people in a small Southern town to survive the depression.

*Rain Man* 1988  MPAA Rating: R
Subject: The relationship between two brothers, one who is autistic.

*Remains of the Day* 1993  MPAA Rating: PG
Subject: The life and culture of the English butler and his devotion to his employer.

*Shadowlands*  1993. See Filmography.

*Shine* 1996  Australia. No Rating.
Subject: The life of a mentally ill concert pianist.

*Untamed Heart*  1993  MPAA Rating: PG-13
Subject: Innocence and love between a young woman and a man with a heart condition.

*What's Eating Gilbert Grape* 1993  MPAA Rating: PG-13
Subject:  The interpersonal relationships of a family plagued by problems but who live life as if they were completely functional. Family members include a retarded son and a 500 lb mother.


## CENTRAL THEME: ROLES OF WOMEN

*A League of Their Own* 1992  MPAA Rating: PG

Subject: Members of a women's softball team face contradictory needs with regard to marriage and family during World War II. Sibling rivalry is also a theme. Some crude language and behavior; alcoholism is a theme.

*Tootsie* 1982  MPAA Rating: PG-13
Subject: Gender issues in the 80s.

## CENTRAL THEME: SEARCH FOR MEANING, WHOLENESS, INTEGRITY

*City Slickers* 1991  MPAA Rating: PG-13
Subject: A man's search for his true purpose in life. Some sexual language and overtones may not be suitable for younger viewers.

*Dead Poets Society** 1989. See Filmography.

*The Neverending Story** 1984. See Filmography.

## CENTRAL THEME: UNIVERSAL TRUTH

*2001: A Space Odyssey* 1968  MPAA Rating: PG
Subject: Space and the meaning of life in a technological society. Themes are intellectual as well as spiritual. Too deep for younger viewers. No objectionable language, sex or nudity. Violence is minimal.

*Mindwalk* 1991  MPAA Rating: PG
Subject: Highly philosophical film involving the discussion between three individuals about the vast questions of life, the

universe and humanity's place in it.  Intellectual, but full of issues for spiritual reflection.

## CENTRAL THEME: URBAN DISCORD

*Boyz n the Hood*** 1991   MPAA Rating: R
Subject: Life in urban Los Angeles.   Themes include gang violence, sex, crude language and repetitive expletives.
Parents should preview.

*Falling Down*** See Filmography.

*Grand Canyon*** 1991  MPAA Rating: R
Subject: Urban reality. Themes include violence, graphic depiction of a shooting, child abandonment, fear and alienation, family love, and friendship between races.

# APPENDIX C

## ADDITIONAL FILM TECHNIQUES
## AND TERMINOLOGY

Definition, description and examples for review


Crosscutting:  Alternating two montage sequences in order to have one inform the meaning of the other.

Dissolve:  An optical device whereby two shots are superimposed as one shot fades out and another shot fades in.  The technique is a transitional editing device indicating a break in temporal continuity (time).  For an example of dissolves see: *Empire of the Sun*--Shanghai harbor, shows two sequential dissolves; *Age of Innocence*.

Fade:  A transitional devise in which an image gradually dims until the viewer sees only a black screen (fade-out) or an image slowly emerges from a black screen to a clear and bright picture (fade-in).  A fade provides a strong break in continuity, usually setting off sequences.  Some directors use white outs and color outs as well, which have the same transitional effect but are more artistic and create a different mood.  See *Age of Innocence* for white and color outs, *The Spitfire Grill* for fades to black.

Iris:  A technique used to show an image in only one small round area of the screen.  A transitional device or a way of focusing attention on a specific part of a scene.  See *The Sting*.

Montage:        A method of editing, originated by Russian
                filmmaker Sergei Eisenstein, in which dissimilar
                materials are juxtaposed to make a statement. See
                *Potemkin*, Odessa Steps sequence.  American
                directors do not use montage in the same way.
                They usually use short shots in sequence to
                reduce the time, increase suspense, allude to
                memory or stream of consciousness.

                For the more advanced reader, look at montage
                and mise-en-scene as complementary forms for
                creating meaning in a film.  Filmmakers can
                create meaning through short shots which are
                edited next to each other (montage) or through the
                composition of the individual shot (mise-en-scene:
                props, lighting, position and posture of actors,
                setting, and point of view of the camera).  Take a
                look at *Age of Innocence*.  Watch for some type
                of montage and replay it for meaning; then look
                at a single shot not in a montage sequence where
                you can study the composition within the frame.
                Note the differences; yet notice they both convey
                important information about the film's themes.

Voice-over:     Words spoken off-screen. The thoughts of
                characters are voiced in *Out of Africa, Havana, A
                River Runs Through It. Age of Innocence* provides
                an example of strict narration by an objective
                party who is not a character.

Wipe:           A transitional device which moves across the
                screen to break continuity.  See *The Sting*.

Zooms:          A quick lens movement toward or away from an
                actor or action, i.e., zoom-in and zoom-out. See
                *The Sting* and *Dances With Wolves*.

# APPENDIX D

## FILMOGRAPHY
### (Arranged Alphabetically)

*Age of Innocence* 138 minutes. 1993.

**MPAA Rating: PG. No sex, violence, nudity or objectionable language.**

While the film's themes evolve around divorce, infidelity, and passionate love, they are discreetly handled and the outcome of the film supports the virtues of the characters rather than their desires.

Columbia Pictures. Dir.: Martin Scorcese. Prod.: Barbara DiFina. Screenplay: Jay Cocks and Martin Scorcese. Based on the novel by Edith Wharton. Cast: Daniel Day-Lewis, Michelle Pfeiffer, Winona Rider, Geraldine Chaplin, Mary Beth Hurt, Miriam Margolyes, Richard Grant, Alex McCowen. Narrated by Joanne Woodward.

*Dead Man Walking* 122 minutes. 1996.

**MPAA Rating: R.  Rape, murder, execution by lethal injection, brief nudity and language. Extreme caution should be exercised in the screening of this film, but older teens and adults should discover much value within it especially in terms of social justice and redemption.**

Some may view the rape and murder of the victims as gratuitous, although Tim Robbins did not belabor the scenes beyond their necessary explication.  I would not recommend this

film to anyone who finds rape or cold-blooded murder or
execution intolerable to view.  The themes of forgiveness and
redemption are so powerfully enacted that the violence is
tolerable.  The death penalty is examined from multiple
perspectives which brings a much-needed educative element to
the controversial issue.  The performances by Susan Sarandon,
as the Catholic nun who serves as the link between the murderer
and his salvation, and Sean Penn, who portrays the accused, are
outstanding.

Dir.: Tim Robbins. Screenplay: Tim Robbins.  From the book
by Sister Helen Prejean. Cast: Susan Sarandon, Sean Penn.


*Dead Poets Society* 128 minutes. 1989.

**MPAA Rating: PG.  Suicide which is not shown, smoking,
high school drinking, a brief Playboy photo of a nude
woman, one scene of corporal punishment inflicted on a
student by the headmaster.  No sex.**

Highly recommended for teens and adults.  The values balance
the negative elements, and the suicide is important to the
overview of the film's worth.  The objectification and moronic
treatment of women is the most unhealthy aspect of the film -- a
good opportunity for parental discussion.  Stereotyping is also
prevalent.

Dir.: Peter Weir.  Sc.: Tom Schulman.  Prod.: Steven Haft,
Paul Junger Witt, Tony Thomas.  Prod. Mgr.: Duncan
Henderson.  Prod. Des.: Wendy Stites.  Music: Maurice Jarre.
Dir. of Photo.: John Seale.  Art Dir.: Sandy Veneziano.  Set
Des.: Carlton Reynolds.  Editing: William Anderson.

Distributed by Touchstone Pictures. Cast: Robin Williams,
Robert Sean Leonard, Ethan Hawke.

*Empire of the Sun* 154 minutes. 1987.

**MPAA RATING: PG.  War, violence, depiction of life in an
internment camp, brief sexual activity, no nudity or
objectionable language.**

Highly recommended for junior high through adult.

Dir.: Steven Spielberg.  Sc.: Tom Stoppard. Based on the novel
by J.G. Ballard.  Prod.: Steven Spielberg, Kathleen Kennedy,
Frank Marshall.  Prod. Mgr.: Ted Morley.  Prod. Des.:
Norman Reynolds.  Music: John Williams.  Dir. of Photo.:
Allen Daviau.  Art Dir.: Frederick Hole.  Editing: Michael
Kahn.  Costume Des.: Bob Ringwood.  Sound: Charles
Campbell.  Distributed by Warner Brothers.  Cast: John
Malkovich, Miranda Richardson, Nigel Havers, Christian Bale.

*Falling Down* 113 minutes. 1993.

**MPAA Rating: R. Violence and language. No sexuality.**

The author encourages parents to view this film prior to
watching it with their children due to its mature content.
Nevertheless, under a parent's guidance the film is extremely
valuable in its depiction of urban reality.  Themes include gang
violence, white supremacist propaganda, ethnic intolerance,
alienation and obsolescence.

Distributed by Warner Brothers. Director: Joel Schumacher.
Screenplay: Ebbe Roe Smith. Producers: Arnold Kopelson,
Herschel Weingrod, Timothy Harris. Production Manager:
William S. Beasley. Production Design: Barbara Ling. Music:
James Newton Howard. Director of Photography: Andrzej
Bartkowiak. Art Director: Larry Fulton. Editing: Paul Hirsch.
Costume Design: Marlene Stewart. **Cast**: Michael Douglas,
Robert Duvall, Barbara Hershey, Tuesday Weld, Rachel
Ticotin, Frederic Forrest.

*The Neverending Story* 92 minutes. 1984. Germany.

**MPAA Rating: PG. Some violence and destruction which
may be frightening to small children; a wolf-like character
representing evil. Many unique fantasy characters which
would require guidance by parents for small children.**

As with all stories which depict good versus evil, *The
Neverending Story* contains some violent and evil elements
which are necessary for the advancement of the story. They are
not gratuitous and there is no sex, nudity or objectionable
language.

Distributed by Warner Brothers. Dir.: Wolfgang Petersen. Sc.:
Wolfgang Petersen and Herman Weigel. Prod.: Bernd
Eichinger and Dieter Geissler. Prod. Mgr.: Harry Nap. Prod.
Des.: Rolf Zehetbauer. Music: Klaus Doldinger and Giorgio
Moroder. Dir. of Photo.: Jost Vacano. Conceptual Artist.: Ul
De Rico. Dir. of Special and Visual Effects: Brian Johnson.
Editing: Jane Seitz. Costume Des.: D. Remy. Sound: Mike Le
Mare. Cast: Noah Hathaway, Barret Oliver, Tami Stronach,

Patricia Hayes, Sydney Bromley, Gerald McRaney, Moses Gunn.


*Nobody's Fool* 110 minutes. 1995.

**MPAA Rating: R.  Partial nudity and sexual references, drinking, gambling, divorce, child abandonment.  Some sporadic crude language may be objectionable to some viewers.**

Highly recommended for its intelligent insights into relationships.  Themes include child-parent love, sibling rivalry, friendship, obligation to family and friends, one's role as a member of a community. Outstanding performances by Paul Newman and Jessica Tandy.

Paramount Pictures. Exec. Prod: Michael Hausman. Prods.: Scott Rudin, Arlene Donovan. Written for the screen and directed: Robert Benton. Based on the novel by Richard Russo. Cast: Paul Newman, Jessica Tandy, Melanie Griffith, Bruce Willis.


*Out of Africa* 161 minutes. 1985.

**MPAA Rating: PG.  Depiction of animal attacks.  Otherwise no violence or objectionable language.  Mild sexual situations and inferences.  Brief native partial nudity; one mild sex scene.**

Highly recommended love story for teens and adults.  Themes include British colonialism in East Africa, ownership, obligation, unconditional love, personal need versus the collective need.

Universal Pictures.  Prod. and dir. by: Sydney Pollack.  Co-Prod.: Terry Clegg.  Exec. Prod.: Kim Jorgensen.  Assoc. Prod.: Judith Thurman and Anna Cataldi. Screenplay: Kurt Luedtke (and David Rayfiel non-credited) based on the book *Out of Africa*, *Letters From Africa*, *Shadows on the Grass* by Isak Dinesen and *Isak Dinesen: the Life of a Storyteller* by Judith Thurman, and *Silence Will Speak* by Errol Trzebinski.  Prod. Mgr.: Gerry Levy.  Prod. Des.: Stephen Grimes.  Music: John Barry.  Dir. of Photo.: David Watkin.  Cast: Meryl Streep, Robert Redford, Klaus Maria Brandauer.

*Searching for Bobby Fischer* 110 minutes. 1993.

**MPAA Rating: PG.  No sex, violence, nudity or objectionable language.**

Strongly recommended for all ages, although young children might not follow the story.

Paramount Pictures. Prods: Scott Rudin, William Horberg. Exec, Prod.: Sydney Pollack. Written and directed by: Steve Zaillian.  Based upon the book by Fred Waitzkin. Cast: Joan Allen, Max Pomeranc, Joe Mantegna, Ben Kingsley, Lawrence Fishburne.

*Shadowlands* 133 minutes. 1993.  UK

**MPAA Rating: PG. No violence, sex, nudity; brief profanity.**

Most suitable for teens and adults.  Depiction of cancer, its treatment and death are the most difficult themes.  Otherwise it is philosophical and powerful in its examination of the meaning of love.

Distributed by Savoy Films. Dir.: Richard Attenborough  Sc.: William Nicholson.  Prod.: Richard Attenborough and Brian Eastman.  Prod. Mgr.: Terence Clegg.  Prod. Des.: Stuart Craig.  Music: George Fenton.  Dir of Photo.: Roger Pratt. Art Dir.: John King.  Editing: Lesley Walker.  Costume Des.: Penny Rose.  Sound: Simon Kaye, Jonathon Bates, Gerry Humphreys.   Cast: Anthony Hopkins, Debra Winger, Edward Hardwicke. Joseph Mazzello, John Wood, Michael Denison.

# BIBLIOGRAPHY


Center for Media and Values literature. Los Angeles, CA.

Considine, David M. and Haley, Gail E. *Visual Messages: Integrating Imagery into Instruction*. Englewood, Colorado: Teacher Ideas Press, 1992.

Ebert, Roger. Review of *Age of Innocence*. *Cinemania '95* on CD-rom, 1995.

Giannetti, Louis. *Understanding Movies*. Englewood Cliffs, N.J.: Prentice Hall, 1976.

Peck, M. Scott. *The Road Less Traveled*. New York: Simon and Schuster, 1978.

Rayfiel, David. *Out of Africa*. Screenplay. 1985.

Robinson, W.R., ed. *Man and the Movies*. Baltimore: Penguin, 1969.

# INDEX